P-AI-R Programming
How AI tools like GitHub Copilot and ChatGPT Can Radically Transform Your Development Workflow

Michael D. Callaghan

Copyright © 2023 Michael D. Callaghan

All rights reserved.

No part of this book may be reproduced, stored in a retrieval system, or transmitted in any form or by any means, electronic, mechanical, photocopying, recording, or otherwise, without the prior written permission of the publisher, except for brief quotations used in critical articles and reviews.

Requests for permission to reproduce material from this book should be directed to michael@walkingriver.com.

This book is sold subject to the condition that it shall not, by way of trade or otherwise, be lent, resold, hired out, or otherwise circulated without the publisher's prior consent in any form of binding or cover other than that in which it is published and without a similar condition, including this condition, being imposed on the subsequent purchaser.

While every effort has been made to ensure the accuracy of the information contained in this book, the author and publisher make no representations or warranties, express or implied, about the completeness, accuracy, reliability, suitability or availability with respect to the information, products, services, or related graphics contained in the book for any purpose. Any reliance you place on such information is therefore strictly at your own risk.

In no event will the author or publisher be liable for any loss or damage including without limitation, indirect or consequential loss or damage, or any loss or damage whatsoever arising from loss of data or profits arising out of, or in connection with, the use of this book.

If you find any errors or inaccuracies, please contact the publisher.

Cover design by Michael D. Callaghan

Preface

About This Book

This book is to designed to be a fun, easy-to-read, and hands-on exploration of using Artificial Intelligence tools as your "pair programming" partner. Throughout the book, I hope you'll see how you can use AI tools like GitHub Copilot and ChatGPT to make your own tasks easier and more effective.

Over the length of the book, we'll cover the following topics:

- Using AI in Software Development
- Shell Scripting Commands
- Git Commands
- Common Algorithms
- Learning RxJS
- Angular's HttpClient
- Regular Expressions
- Data Generation
- Agile Project Management
- Let's Build an App!
- Unit Testing
- Other Considerations
- The Future of Software Development

My goal is to inspire you to come up with your own ideas and vastly improve your efficiency.

Who is This Book For?

This book is for any software developer of any level, from "just starting out" to "ready to retire." Though most of my examples use specific web technologies like HTML, JavaScript, TypeScript, and Ionic, you don't need to be familiar with these languages and frameworks to get something out of this book.

Following Along

Regardless of the type of software development you do, I'm sure you'll find value by following along in whatever language you prefer.

I'm pleased to offer you a list of most of the prompts I use throughout the book, in case you want to follow along and don't want to type them. You can sign up and download them free of charge here:

https://walkingriver.gumroad.com/l/pair-programming-bonus

Updates and Questions

If you ever have questions or just want to be updated about this and future books, feel free to sign up at the link above, or send an email to michael@walkingriver.com.

I'm also very active on Twitter, where you can find me posting as @WalkingRiver.

Books on Amazon

You can find the rest of my titles on Amazon at https://amazon.com/author/mcallaghan.

If you enjoy this book, I'd appreciate you leaving me a positive review on Amazon, which you can do here: https://www.amazon.com/review/create-review?asin=B0BSNZFCRM

P-AI-R Programming

Copyright © 2023 by Michael D. Callaghan. All rights reserved.

No part of this book may be reproduced, stored in a retrieval system, or transmitted in any form or by any means, electronic, mechanical, photocopying, recording, or otherwise, without the prior written permission of the publisher, except for brief quotations used in critical articles and reviews.

Requests for permission to reproduce material from this book should be directed to michael@walkingriver.com.

This book is sold subject to the condition that it shall not, by way of trade or otherwise, be lent, resold, hired out, or otherwise circulated without the publisher's prior consent in any form of binding or cover other than that in which it is published and without a similar condition, including this condition, being imposed on the subsequent purchaser.

While every effort has been made to ensure the accuracy of the information contained in this book, the author and publisher make no representations or warranties, express or implied, about the completeness, accuracy, reliability, suitability or availability with respect to the information, products, services, or related graphics contained in the book for any purpose. Any reliance you place on such information is therefore strictly at your own risk.

In no event will the author or publisher be liable for any loss or damage including without limitation, indirect or consequential loss or damage, or any loss or damage whatsoever arising from loss of data or profits arising out of, or in connection with, the use of this book.

If you find any errors or inaccuracies, please contact the publisher.

Cover design by Michael D. Callaghan

USING AI IN SOFTWARE DEVELOPMENT

Image by Gerd Altmann on Pixabay

I first heard about GitHub Copilot in mid-2022. I was intrigued by the idea that someone trained an Artificial Intelligence (henceforth "AI") model from the source code inside every public GitHub repo. Further, that once the model had been trained, it could essentially understand my source code and make suggestions in real time. If this were real, I had to try it.

I registered for the free beta and waited. About a week later, I got the email accepting me into the beta program, along with a link to install a Visual Studio Code extension. I installed the extension and started playing with it. It seemed cool but I don't do a lot of day-to-day coding on my personal machine and wasn't ready to install Beta software on my work computer. So, I promptly forgot about it for a while.

In June I ran a live mobile app development workshop. For the code demos, I had VS Code running on my personal Mac. Copilot was still installed, and it continued to pop up and offer code completion suggestions. Finally, someone asked what it was, so we went off on a tangent and spent some time exploring Copilot's capabilities. It seemed to know what code should be written before we did. We were all impressed, to say the least.

It seemed to know all about Ionic and Angular, HTML, CSS, and TypeScript. It understood those languages in the context of the demo app I was building for the workshop. It was rarely wrong, providing code nearly identical to what I was about type.

Fast forward a few months. ChatGPT showed up and took the world by storm. Here was the first "approachable" AI with a conversational interface. People could ask it questions and expect a coherent answer.

Millions of people began experimenting with it, seeing how well it could write code simply by entering a brief description of the problem. While not perfect, its answers were surprisingly good. People began wondering whether we had entered a strange new world of software development, one where traditional coding, and software developers, would soon be obsolete.

What We Will Cover

My objective in writing this book is to describe how AI can be used in the day-to-day activities of a typical software developer. Before we dive deep into these concepts, let's take a high-level look at what the tools can and cannot do for us.

What Can AI Tools Do?

1. Code generation: AI can be used to generate code based on a set of inputs and requirements, which can speed up the development process and reduce the chance of errors.
2. Test automation: AI can be used to automatically generate test cases and test scripts, which can save time and improve the quality of software.
3. Quality assurance: AI can be used to automatically evaluate the quality of code, which can help identify potential issues before they become problems.
4. UI/UX design: AI can be used to generate UI/UX designs, which can save

time and improve the overall user experience.
   5. Language Processing: AI can be used for natural language processing, which can be used in natural language interface for software development.
   6. Predictive analytics: AI can be used to predict future trends, bugs and areas that need attention.
   7. AI-powered search: AI can be used to search and recommend relevant code snippets, libraries and tools to developers.

I will be focusing on the first two items in that list, as they seem most relevant to software development today.

What are Their Limitations?

   1. Limited understanding of context: AI may not fully understand the context in which code is being written, which can lead to errors or inconsistencies.
   2. Lack of creativity: AI can generate code or designs that are functional but may lack the creativity of a human developer.
   3. Limited ability to handle complexity: AI may struggle with complex code or designs that involve many variables and interdependencies.
   4. Lack of understanding of industry standards and best practices: AI may not be aware of the best practices and standards in a particular industry or field, which can lead to suboptimal results.
   5. Lack of flexibility: AI may not be able to adapt to changing requirements or unexpected situations as well as a human developer.
   6. Limited ability to handle unstructured data: AI may struggle with data that is not well-organized or does not conform to a specific format.
   7. Limited ability to generalize: AI may struggle to generalize from examples and may not work well in situations where it has not been explicitly trained.
   8. Data bias: AI models can perpetuate human biases if the training data is not diverse and representative of the population.
   9. Dependence on large amounts of data: AI models often require large amounts of data to be trained, which can be difficult to acquire and process.
   10. Lack of explainability: AI models can be opaque, making it difficult to understand how they arrived at a particular decision or output. As we will see, this is where ChatGPT shines.

Different AIs Used in This Book

There are a lot of AI tools that we could choose. I won't pretend to know even half of them. The two with the biggest market penetration and clout seem to be ChatGPT from OpenAI and Copilot from GitHub. Those are the two I will focus on throughout the book.

ChatGPT

ChatGPT is a language model developed by OpenAI. It is a variant of the GPT (Generative Pre-trained Transformer) model, which is trained on a massive amount of internet text data to generate human-like text. The model is fine-tuned for specific tasks, such as language translation, text summarization, and conversation. With its ability to understand and respond to natural language inputs, ChatGPT can be used for a variety of applications, such as chatbots, virtual assistants, and language-based games.

People discovered very quickly that it can also be used to generate functioning computer code in a variety of languages. ChatGPT, as a powerful language generation model, can be used in several ways to help with software development:

1. Code generation: ChatGPT can be used to generate code snippets and even complete functions based on a set of inputs and requirements, which can speed up the development process and reduce the chance of errors.
2. Text generation: ChatGPT can be used to generate comments, documentation and even commit messages, which can save developers time and improve code readability.
3. Test case generation: ChatGPT can be used to generate test cases and test scripts for software, which can save time and improve the quality of software.

To use ChatGPT, you will need to sign up for an OpenAI API account, which you can do at https://chat.openai.com/chat. If you already have an account with OpenAI, you can log in with that. If not, you will need to register.

At the time of this writing, there are two tiers to the service: one is free, but you may find that it is frequently "at capacity," which makes it hard to use.

There is also a paid tier, ChatGPT PLUS, which is currently $20USD per month. OpenAI has also announced plans for additional tiers, as well as a waitlist so you can get more information.

GitHub Copilot

Copilot is an AI-powered coding assistant developed by GitHub. It is a system that aims to help developers write code more efficiently and effectively by suggesting code completions. Copilot uses machine learning to understand the code you're working on, and suggests completions based on the context of the code, taking into account the structure of the repository and the contents of the file you're working on. Copilot suggests completions for variables, functions, and more, based on the context of the code you're working on.

The tool can be used to generate code snippets, complete function calls and arguments, and suggest variable and function names. Copilot can be used with multiple programming languages such as Python, JavaScript, and Go, and it can be integrated with popular code editors such as Visual Studio Code, Atom, and Sublime Text. Throughout this book, I'll be using it exclusively inside VS Code.

One of the key features of GitHub Copilot is its ability to understand the developer's intent. This means that it can not only suggest code snippets, but also understand the problem that the developer is trying to solve and provide suggestions accordingly. For example, if a developer is trying to write a function to sort a list of numbers, Copilot will understand that the developer is trying to sort the list and will provide suggestions for sorting algorithms. One of my personal blind spots is in writing reducers in JavaScript. Copilot has gotten them right for me every time I've tried.

Sometimes, Copilot will offer multiple possibilities. If you aren't happy with the code Copilot initially suggests, you can cycle through multiple suggestions with Opt + [and Opt +] on macOS or Alt + [and Alt +] on Windows and Linux.

Another important feature of GitHub Copilot is its ability to learn from the developer's codebase. As the you write your code, Copilot will learn about your coding style, and will use this information to provide more accurate and relevant suggestions. This means that the more you use Copilot, the more it will understand your coding preferences and will improve its suggestions.

GitHub Copilot also uses GitHub's vast codebase to learn from the best practices and patterns of other developers. It can leverage the knowledge from open-source code and from the contributions of the developer's own team to provide suggestions that are in line with the best practices of the community.

To use Copilot, you will need to sign up at https://github.com/features/copilot.

GitHub Copilot was free to use while it was in Beta, but now that it's been officially released, it requires a license. At the time of this writing, Copilot is $100/year per developer. There is a free trial, in case you want to follow along with the book before you decide whether to subscribe. Students and open-source maintainers can still use it free of charge, but you have to apply and wait to be approved.

ChatGPT vs Copilot

ChatGPT and GitHub Copilot are both AI-powered tools that are designed to assist software developers in their work. Both tools use machine learning algorithms to provide developers with intelligent suggestions and assistance, but they are designed for different aspects of the development process.

One of the main differences between the two tools is their area of focus. ChatGPT is focused on natural language processing tasks, while GitHub Copilot is focused on code completion and suggestions. ChatGPT can be used to generate text responses or code, while GitHub Copilot can be used primarily to generate code snippets.

Another difference is the way the two tools are used. ChatGPT is accessed through a chat-like interface (hence the name), so developers tend to be more descriptive in using it to generate code. On the other hand, GitHub Copilot is integrated into the development environment and can be used directly inside your project.

Throughout the book, I will use both tools to highlight how they can be used most effectively in the proper situation.

Controversy - Should Developers Use These Tools?

I thought I should get this out of the way early because there are those who feel the answer is a definite "no."

One of the main complaints arising from Copilot's use of GitHub's codebase to train its model and make its suggestions is that it could lead to the spread of bad coding practices and security vulnerabilities. Since the tool is using the codebase to learn from the practices and patterns of other developers, it may inadvertently be learning and promoting bad coding practices and security vulnerabilities that exist in those codebases. This could lead to developers unknowingly incorporating these issues into their own code, potentially leading to security breaches or other problems.

Another potential issue is that Copilot could undermine the importance of understanding and knowledge of the codebase; developers may become too reliant on the tool's suggestions and not take the time to understand the code they are working on. This could lead to developers not fully understanding the codebase, making it more difficult to maintain and troubleshoot issues in the future.

Furthermore, Copilot's use of GitHub's codebase to train its model also raises concerns about privacy and data security. As the tool is analyzing and learning from code written by developers, it may also be collecting and analyzing sensitive data, such as usernames, passwords, or other personal information.

Licensing Issues

One of the larger criticisms and causes of the controversy stem from licensing issues with the data used to train the AI models. This can be a significant concern, as using code without proper permission or licensing can lead to legal issues. Some specific issues that can arise include:

1. Copyright infringement if the data used to train an AI model is protected by copyright.
2. Trade secret infringement if the data used to train an AI model constitutes someone else's trade secret.
3. If the data used to train an AI model contains personal information, using it without proper permission or anonymizing it may violate privacy laws.
4. If the data used to train an AI model is subject to a license or contract, using it in a way that violates those terms can lead to legal issues.

It's important for developers and organizations to be aware of these issues and to obtain proper permissions and licenses for any data used to train AI models. This can include obtaining licenses for open-source datasets or negotiating agreements with data providers to use proprietary data.

No Respecter of Licenses

When using AI to help write software, it is important to consider the open-source licenses of the code that may have been used to train the AI. Open-source licenses are agreements that dictate how the code covered by the license can be used, modified, and distributed. Different open-source licenses have different terms and conditions, so it is important to carefully review the licenses of any code that is used to train the AI and ensure that they are being complied with. This may involve obtaining the proper permissions, giving credit to the original authors, and making any required changes to the code. Failing to properly comply with open-source licenses can result in legal consequences, such as being sued for copyright infringement.

A concrete example may illustrate the issue more clearly. In one of my mobile apps,

I use an algorithm I found to generate a deck of cards of an arbitrary size. The JavaScript code I found on GitHub (not using Copilot) is clearly marked as "GPL Licensed." As I understand it (and I'm not a lawyer), this means that I am free to use this algorithm in my own code, and can even sell the app. That's allowed. However, I must include the GPL notice in the source code. I must also release my source code under the same license.

What if Copilot had suggested this algorithm to me and I was unaware of its license, and then proceeded to offer my app under a different license? Would I technically be in violation of the GPL from the original algorithm? If so, what risk would this expose me or my employer to? Unfortunately, these types of questions will probably need to be settled in courts. As I write this, there is at least one lawsuit pending regarding Copilot's use of licensed software in its recommendations.

Ethical Considerations

What are the ethics of using AI to help with software development? Is it ethical to use an AI to help write software? Can the developer or company really claim that they are the proper authors of said software? This may seem odd, but I asked ChatGPT that very question. This is how it replied.

> It is generally considered ethical to use AI to assist in the development of software, as long as the developers and the company are transparent about the role of the AI in the development process and give credit where it is due. The developer or company can claim authorship of the software but should also acknowledge the contributions of the AI used in the development process. Additionally, it is important to ensure that any AI models used in the development of software are trained on ethically sourced data and do not perpetuate any biases.

I also asked it whether there are any other ethical considerations to be aware of.

> First, there is the issue of fairness and bias. It is important to ensure that the AI system is not making decisions based on biased data, as this could result in unfair treatment of certain individuals or groups. Additionally, there is the question of accountability. It is important to consider who is responsible for any errors or mistakes made by the AI system, and to ensure that there are appropriate safeguards in place to prevent such errors from happening. Finally, there is the issue of privacy. It is important to ensure that the personal data of users is collected, used, and stored in a manner that respects their privacy and complies with relevant laws and regulations.

Conventions Used in This Book

As you see above, I am adopting the convention of printing the output from the AI in a different font and background, so that you can easily see distinguish my thoughts from the AI's.

> *When I show a comment or prompt get Copilot to generate code, I will show it like this.*
>
> *When I show a comment or prompt get ChatGPT to generate code, I will show it like this.*
>
> Output used verbatim from ChatGPT will be shown this way.
>
> Also, any commands or generated source code will be shown this way.

SHELL SCRIPTING COMMANDS

Image by cocoandwifi from Pixabay

Shell scripting is a fundamental skill for anyone who wants to efficiently manage and automate tasks on a computer.

Let's investigate how Copilot and ChatGPT do with shell scripting. A while back I wrote an article about what these symbols (~|&||&&$!`()?) mean in a bash (or similar) shell and how to use them.

Can GitHub Copilot and ChatGPT give me these types of commands from nothing but comments? Read on to find out.

#!/bin/bash

Copilot only works in the context of a code editor. It has no conversational interface as ChatGPT does. Thus, to test Copilot, the first thing I did was to create a blank file in VS Code. At the top of the file, I added a "shebang" line to indicate that the file contains shell scripting code.

```
#!/bin/bash
```

Next, I added the following comment to see what Copilot would write for me.

```
# Check for a directory and print a message if it doesn't exist
```

To my surprise, it didn't do anything. Maybe, I thought, Copilot doesn't know about shell scripting and this experiment will end quickly. Then it hit me. It didn't get the hint from the shebang, but probably from the file extension. I saved the file as copilot.sh and tried again.

This time, Copilot gave me some code.

```
if [ ! -d /home/username/Downloads ]; then
    echo "The directory /home/username/Downloads does not exist."
fi
```

It isn't what I expected, but it does what the comment says.

File Extension?

As I mentioned, Copilot needs to know what kind of file it is before it can write code for you. Through further experimentation, I discovered that it isn't the file extension that made Copilot understand the file type. Instead, it was VS Code itself. Saving the file with a .sh extension told VS Code that it was a Shell Script file.

```
Ln 1, Col 1    Spaces: 2    UTF-8    LF    Plain Text
```

The file extension is less important than the type of file VS Code thinks it is. In most cases, VS Code gets it right automatically. If not, you can click on the phrase "Plain Text" in the bottom status bar. A menu will appear at the top of the page, allowing you to select the file type manually.

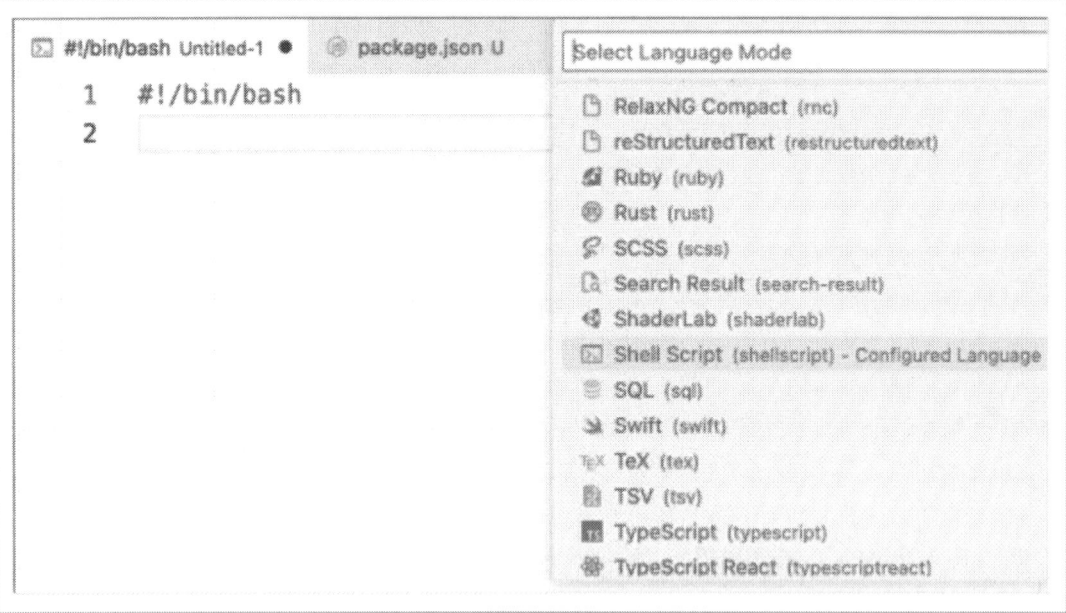

In my case, saving the file with a .sh did the trick. In another instance, adding the "Shebang" line did it. The results seemed inconsistent, so double-check the type.

The important thing to remember is that Copilot only cares about that file type and not the extension.

What about ChatGPT?

ChatGPT seems better suited for these sorts of things, given its more conversational nature. Here is how it responded to the same prompt:

Check for a directory and print a message if it doesn't exist

You can use the **test** command (also known as [or [[) to check if a directory exists, and the **echo** command to print a message if it doesn't. Here is an example:

if test ! -d /path/to/directory; then

    echo "Directory does not exist"

fi

Alternatively, you could use the **if [! -d "/path/to/directory"]; then** command with the same echo message.

Another option is to use if [[! -d "/path/to/directory"]]; then

The difference between the two sets of output is immediately apparent. ChatGPT offers an explanation with its answers, and does not simply give you the code. As you will see, this can be a significant advantage to using ChatGPT over Copilot.

The find Command

The next thing I tried was to find all the PDF files anywhere in my home directory and below. Normally when I do that, I use the `find` command. Is that what Copilot would suggest? I entered the following comment:

```
# Find all PDF files in my home directory and print the path to each one
```

When I pressed the Return key, nothing happened. I tried a few more times, but Copilot refused to suggest anything. Then I decided to try to give it a hint. I typed the word find on a line by itself, just beneath that comment. Copilot immediately sprang to life and suggested the following completion:

```
find /home/username -name "*.pdf" -print
```

I was a little disappointed. That command won't work unless my home directory just happens to be /home/username. However, then I started thinking about it. Copilot did the hard part. It got the syntax of the find command correct. I can always edit it to fix my home directory.

In fact, when I changed my hint to `find ~`, it did the right thing with no further aid.

If you are not aware, `~` is a shell short cut meaning "my account's home directory."

ChatGPT gave me two different options.

Find all PDF files in my home directory and print the path to each one

You can use the **find** command to search for all PDF files in your home directory and print the path to each one. Here's an example:

```
find ~ -name "*.pdf" -print
```

This will search for all files in your home directory (~) that end in **.pdf** and print the path to each one.

Alternatively, you could use **ls** command with wildcard,

```
ls ~/ -R | grep .pdf$
```
This will recursively list all files in your home directory, and filter only the files with .pdf extension.

As I expected, ChatGPT does a much better job than Copilot. As before, I appreciate that it provides an explanation and not just the command. If you are trying to learn, this is the better experience.

Background Tasks

The next thing I wanted to do was to determine whether the AI knows how to use some of those symbols that often trip up beginners. Would they know that the greater than sign (`>`) is used to redirect output and that the ampersand (`&`) is used to run a command in the background?

I changed my comment as follows, and then gave it the same hint from above.

```
# Find all PDF files below my home folder and write the results to a file called pdfs.txt in the background.
find ~ -name "*.pdf" > pdfs.txt &
```

That's exactly right, though I was confused that it dropped the `-print` parameter. Then I remembered that printing is the default behavior of the find command.

As before, ChatGPT gave me multiple options, complete with thorough explanations.

Find all PDF files below my home folder and write the results to a file called pdfs.txt in the background.

You can use the **find** command to search for all PDF files below your home directory, and the **tee** command to write the results to a file called pdfs.txt in the background. Here's an example:

```
find ~ -name "*.pdf" -print | tee pdfs.txt &
```

This will search for all files in your home directory and its subdirectories that end in **.pdf** and print the path to each one. The output will be piped to the **tee** command, which will write it to a file called pdfs.txt in the current directory. The **&** at the end will run the command in background, so you can continue to use the terminal.

Alternatively, you could use **ls** command with wildcard,

```
ls ~/ -R | grep .pdf$ >> pdfs.txt &
```

This will recursively list all files in your home directory and its subdirectories, and filter only the files with .pdf extension, and write it to pdfs.txt file. The **&** at the end will run the command in background as well.

I had forgotten all about the `tee` command. I'm also impressed that it went a little farther with the `ls` command, using `grep` with a simple regular expression to find files that end in `.pdf`. It also assumed I would want to append to my `pdfs.txt` file if it already exists. Though not exactly what I asked for, it actually gave me more.

Output Pipe

Next, I wanted to see whether they know how to use the output of one command as the input to another. I was also curious to know whether they are aware of the previous command just generated. Do they remember?

Here is my Copilot comment and the command it generated.

```
# Count the number of PDF files in my home folder in the background and print the result.
find ~ -name "*.pdf" | wc -l &
```

I had hoped it would use the file it created from the last command, but it didn't. It did, however, remember that I prefer to use `find ~`.

ChatGPT again gave me multiple options.

> *Count the number of PDF files in my home folder in the background and print the result.*
>
> You can use the **find** command to search for all PDF files in your home directory, and the **wc** command to count the number of files and print the result. Here's an example:
>
> ```
> find ~ -name "*.pdf" -print | wc -l > count.txt &
> ```
>
> This will search for all files in your home directory and its subdirectories that end in **.pdf**, print the path to each one, then pipe the output to the **wc** command with the **-l** option which will count the number of lines and redirect the output to a file called count.txt in the current directory. The **&** at the end will run the command in background, so you can continue to use the terminal.
>
> Alternatively, you could use **ls** command with wildcard:
>
> ```
> ls -R ~/ | grep .pdf$ | wc -l > count.txt &
> ```
>
> This will recursively list all files in your home directory and its subdirectories, filter only the files with .pdf extension, pipe the output to the **wc** command with the **-l** option which will count the number of lines and redirect the output to a file called count.txt in the current directory. The **&** at the end will run the command in background as well.

At this point, I found myself wondering whether it ever makes sense to use Copilot for the command line. I continued to do so for the rest of these tests.

Redirect Errors to Ignore Them

Most people know how to use the `>` character to redirect the output of a command to a file. If the command encounters any errors, those will still display in the terminal, which can be confusing when running the command in the background.

I know it is possible to redirect errors to a special file called `/dev/null`, so that they are ignored completely. Unfortunately, I can never remember the syntax. I don't know why because it isn't that complicated. It's one of my weird blind spots, I suppose.

Fortunately, Copilot knows exactly how to do it. I decided to combine some of the above concepts to see what it would do. It got it right on the first try.

```
# Find all the PDF files below my home folder, in the background, ignoring errors, and write the output to a file.
find ~ -name "*.pdf" > pdfs.txt 2> /dev/null &
```

ChatGPT Remembers

What's really cool about ChatGPT is that it remembers earlier parts of your conversation. For this one, I changed up the prompt and simply asked it to "rewrite the last command to ignore any errors." The explanations are almost identical as those it provided above, so I'll spare you the duplication and simply show you the commands it gave me. Again, it gave me two options.

Option 1 – Find

```
find ~ -name "*.pdf" -print 2> /dev/null | wc -l > count.txt &
```

Option 2 – ls

```
ls -R ~/ 2> /dev/null | grep .pdf$ | wc -l > count.txt &
```

*nix System Administration

I started wondering whether they could help me with some common system administration tasks, such as creating users, adding users to groups, and so forth.

Add a New User Account

I decided to start with something simple, so I asked Copilot to create a new user account for me.

```
# Create a new user account
sudo adduser username
```

This doesn't work on a Mac. Maybe it works on Linux. I decided to try again and got this.

```
# Create a new user account on macos
dscl . -create /Users/username
```

Running that gave me a permission error. I tried once again, prepending `sudo` to the command. That one might have worked; I'm not sure. The folder `/Users/username` does not exist, nor did a user by that name appear when I opened the Users control panel. Maybe I'm still missing something.

This is an example where Copilot might be more frustrating than helpful.

ChatGPT again outdid itself, providing more detail and explanation.

> *Create a new user account on macos*
>
> To create a new user account on macOS, you can use the dscl (Directory Service command line utility) command. Here is an example of how to create a new user account called "newuser" with a password of "newpassword":
>
> sudo dscl . -create /Users/newuser
>
> sudo dscl . -create /Users/newuser UserShell /bin/bash
>
> sudo dscl . -create /Users/newuser RealName "New User"
>
> sudo dscl . -create /Users/newuser UniqueID "501"
>
> sudo dscl . -create /Users/newuser PrimaryGroupID 20
>
> sudo dscl . -create /Users/newuser NFSHomeDirectory /Users/newuser
>
> sudo dscl . -passwd /Users/newuser newpassword
>
> This creates the account, sets the shell to /bin/bash, sets the RealName, UniqueID, PrimaryGroupID and home directory, and sets the password.
>
> Alternatively, you can use the **sysadminctl** command to create a new user account and set the password. Here is an example:
>
> sudo sysadminctl -addUser newuser -fullName "New User" -password newpassword -admin
>
> This creates the account with the username "newuser", full name "New User", password

> "newpassword" and admin privilege.
>
> You also can use the GUI by going to System Preferences > Users & Groups > click on the lock icon to unlock it > click on the "+" sign to add a new user.
>
> Please note that these commands require administrative privileges and should be used with caution.

I tried the second command on my Mac and it worked flawlessly. ChatGPT wins here handily.

Make an Existing User an Admin

Next, I asked them both for the command to make an existing user an admin.

```
# Make user 'michael' a local administrator
sudo dseditgroup -o edit -a michael -t user admin
```

I'm honestly not sure whether that one will work, but it looks correct. Again, is Copilot being helpful or frustrating?

ChatGPT again gave me a set of options, the second of which matched Copilot's suggestion.

> *Make user 'michael' a local administrator*
>
> To make a user "michael" a local administrator on macOS, you can use the **dscl** (Directory Service command line utility) command. Here is an example of how to make the user "michael" a local administrator:
>
> `sudo dscl . -append /Groups/admin GroupMembership michael`
>
> This command adds the user "michael" to the "admin" group. Members of the "admin" group have administrative privileges on the system.
>
> Alternatively, you can use the **dseditgroup** command to add a user to the "admin" group. Here is an example:
>
> `sudo dseditgroup -o edit -a michael -t user admin`
>
> This command adds the user "michael" to the "admin" group.
>
> You also can use the GUI by going to System Preferences > Users & Groups > click on the lock icon to unlock it > right click on the user you want to change > select "Advanced Options" > change the "Account type" to "Administrator".
>
> Please note that these commands require administrative privileges and should be used with caution.

Backup Files

Have you ever used `rsync` to back up files from one system to another? No? Of course not. No one does (ok, maybe some people do). It's hard to remember the syntax. That's why Dropbox and other such services exist. Maybe Copilot knows the syntax.

```
# Sync my home folder to a remote server
rsync -avz --delete ~/ username@server:/home/username
```

It suffers from the same path name problems from before but again, those are easily recognized and fixed. What isn't so easily discerned is whether those parameters are correct. I did a little research on my Mac using `man rsync` to read the command's online manual. It seems that the command above is exactly what you would want to synchronize the source folder to the destination machine.

The `--delete` parameter tells the command to delete any extra files at the destination that are not on the source. If you just want to copy everything, keeping files on the destination you might have removed locally, you can omit this parameter.

ChatGPT gave me four different suggestions, with `rsync` being the first one. It also suggested using `scp`, which I had planned to ask about next.

> *Sync my home folder to a remote server*
>
> There are several ways to sync your home folder to a remote server on macOS. Here are a few options:
>
> **rsync**: This command-line tool can be used to synchronize files and directories between two locations. Here's an example of how to use **rsync** to sync your home folder to a remote server:
>
> ```
> rsync -avz -e ssh ~/ username@remote-server:/path/to/remote/folder/
> ```
>
> This command will sync all files and directories in your home folder to the specified remote server. The **-a** option tells **rsync** to preserve file permissions and ownership, the **-v** option provides verbose output, and the **-z** option enables compression to speed up the transfer. The **-e** option specifies the remote shell to use, in this case **ssh**.
>
> **scp**: This command-line tool can be used to copy files and directories between a local machine and a remote server. Here's an example of how to use **scp** to sync your home folder to a remote server:
>
> ```
> scp -r ~/ username@remote-server:/path/to/remote/folder/
> ```
>
> This command will copy all files and directories in your home folder to the specified remote server.

The **-r** option tells **scp** to copy directories recursively.

Finder: You also can use Finder to sync your home folder to a remote server by mounting the remote folder as a local volume using SMB, NFS or FTP protocols, and then use the Finder to copy the files and folders.

Third party software: There are also third-party software like ChronoSync, Carbon Copy Cloner, and others that can be used to sync your home folder to a remote server.

Please note that these commands require a remote server with the appropriate permissions and access to be set up, and also make sure you have the correct login credentials to access the remote server.

Securely Copy from Server to Local

Instead of backing up files, maybe there are some files on a remote server that you want to copy locally. You might use a command like this.

```
# Securely Copy from Server to Local folder
scp -r username@server:/home/username/ ~/Downloads
```

Yes, that one is correct, too. ChatGPT had already suggested `scp` as one possible method to synchronize files to a remote server, and I fully expected it to get this one with ease.

Securely Copy from Server to Local folder

To securely copy files from a remote server to a local folder on macOS, you can use the **scp** command. **scp** stands for "secure copy" and it uses the SSH protocol to transfer files.

Here's an example of how to use **scp** to copy a file called "file.txt" from the remote server "remote-server" to the local folder "~/Downloads":

```
scp username@remote-server:/path/to/file.txt ~/Downloads
```

This command will copy the file "file.txt" from the specified path on the remote server to the "Downloads" folder in your home directory.

You can also copy a directory and its contents by adding the -r option, which stands for "recursive"

```
scp -r username@remote-server:/path/to/directory ~/Downloads
```

You can also copy multiple files and directories by listing them, for example:

```
scp username@remote-server:/path/to/file1.txt /path/to/file2.txt /path/to/directory1/ ~/Downloads
```

You also can specify a different port number if the remote server uses a non-default port by using -P option:

```
scp -P 22 username@remote-server:/path/to/file.txt ~/Downloads
```

Please note that these commands require a remote server with the appropriate permissions and access to be set up, and also make sure you have the correct login credentials to access the remote server. Also, the **scp** command encrypts the data as it is transferred, providing an additional layer of security.

Archiving Folders

Sometimes we want to back up a folder by creating an archive. We might want to email it or upload it to a public server, or just simply copy it to a flash drive. If the goal is to keep the files together, an archive is perfect. If only I could remember what that command syntax is.

I gave them both the same prompt, with Copilot first. I asked them each for both the commands to archive and unarchive a given directory.

```
# Archive the src directory using tar and gzip
tar -cvzf src.tar.gz src
# Uncompress the tar.gz file
tar -xvzf src.tar.gz
```

The commands are correct, but again, Copilot provides the information without context. In source code, this makes a lot of sense. If you don't know what the `tar` command does, though, you may still be lost. You certainly won't know that you can safely remove the `v` from the parameter and still get the results you want.

Let's see how ChatGPT did.

Archive the src directory using tar and gzip

To archive the **src** directory using **tar** and **gzip**, you can use the following command:

```
tar -czvf src.tar.gz src/
```

This command creates a new archive file called **src.tar.gz** that contains the contents of the **src** directory. The **-c** option tells **tar** to create a new archive, the **-z** option tells it to use **gzip** to compress the archive, and the **-v** option tells it to display verbose information about the progress of the archive creation. The **-f** option specifies the name and location of the archive file.

You can also use **tar** with **gzip** with the following command

```
tar -zcvf src.tar.gz src/
```

It will produce the same result.

Please note that this command will create the archive file in the current directory, you can specify a different directory to save the archive file. Also, the original **src** directory will not be deleted, if you want to delete it after archiving you can add **--remove-files** option

```
tar -czvf src.tar.gz --remove-files src/
```

This command will archive the src directory and remove the original directory after archiving it.

This is the first time I have seen ChatGPT provide the exact same information as an alternative to its first suggestion. Notice that the first two commands are identical except for the ordering of parameters, which is irrelevant. It's literally the same command.

I do appreciate the third option it gave, though. I was not aware of the `--remove-files` option.

I then asked it to uncompress the tar file. I admit that I was not prepared for the tutorial it generated.

To uncompress a **.tar.gz** file, you can use the following command:

```
tar -xzvf src.tar.gz
```

This command tells **tar** to extract the contents of the **src.tar.gz** file, the **-x** option tells it to extract the archive, the **-z** option tells it to use **gzip** to decompress the archive, and the **-v** option tells it to display verbose information about the progress of the extraction. The **-f** option specifies the name and location of the archive file.

You can also use the following command

```
tar -xvf src.tar.gz
```

This command will also extract the contents of the **src.tar.gz** file, but you need to specify that the file is gzipped by adding the **-z** option

```
tar -xvzf src.tar.gz
```

This command will extract the contents of the archive to the current directory, if you want to extract the files to a different directory you can use the **-C** option

```
tar -xvzf src.tar.gz -C /path/to/directory
```

This command will extract the files to the directory **/path/to/directory**.

> Please note that the extracted files will have the same permissions and ownership as the original files, if you want to change the permissions or ownership of the extracted files you can use the **--no-same-permissions** and **--no-same-owner** options.
>
> ```
> tar -xvzf src.tar.gz --no-same-permissions --no-same-owner
> ```
>
> This command will extract the files with the current user's permissions and ownership.
>
> Also, after extracting the files you can delete the original archive file by adding **-k** option
>
> ```
> tar -xvzf src.tar.gz -k
> ```
>
> This command will extract the files and keep the original archive file.
>
> It's important to note that tar.gz files are also known as tarballs, they are a combination of tar archive and gzip compression, the **.tar** file contains the files and the **.gz** file is the compression. It's important to use both options -x and -z to extract and decompress the file respectively.

Once again, it managed to get confused and essentially gave me the same command for two different options. Otherwise, I think it did a thorough job explaining things.

GitHub SSH Key

I don't know about you, but I always have to look up how to create a new SSH key for GitHub using `git+ssh` protocol. Maybe I could get Copilot to do it for me.

```
# Create and copy a new ssh key for github to the clipboard
ssh-keygen -t rsa -b 4096 -C "
" && cat ~/.ssh/id_rsa.pub | pbcopy
```

This command is correct and exactly what I expected, with the exception of the -C " prompt it gave me. In fact, Copilot stopped after that parameter, as if it expected me to input something.

Whenever Copilot gives you a partial command as its output, it is either waiting for you to enter more info yourself or it wants you to continue on the next line.

As it turns out `-C` is simply a comment to the key, so I could have typed something like `github-key` and continued on. As soon as I pressed `Return`, it gave me the second line. This line tells the shell to copy the public key from my home directory's `.ssh` directory into the clipboard using `pbcopy`.

At that point, the computer's clipboard should have a copy of my public key, which I can then paste into GitHub's public key UI.

ChatGPT suggested that I use my email address as the comment and gave me a complete example. It also split the process into two commands instead a one.

Create and copy a new ssh key for github to the clipboard

To create and copy a new SSH key for use with GitHub on macOS, you can use the **ssh-keygen** and **pbcopy** command. Here is an example of how to create a new SSH key and copy it to the clipboard:

Open the Terminal and generate a new SSH key:

```
ssh-keygen -t rsa -b 4096 -C "your_email@example.com"
```

This command creates a new RSA key with a 4096-bit key size, and associates the email "your_email@example.com" with the key as a comment.

When prompted, you can press Enter to accept the default location and file name for the key, or enter a new location and file name.

After the key is generated, you can copy the key to your clipboard using the **pbcopy** command:

```
pbcopy < ~/.ssh/id_rsa.pub
```

This command copies the contents of the file "~/.ssh/id_rsa.pub" to the clipboard.

Go to your GitHub settings, under SSH and GPG keys, click on "New SSH Key" button.

Give a title to the key, and paste the key on the "Key" field, press "Add SSH key" button.

You can test the connection by running **ssh -T git@github.com**

Please note that **pbcopy** command only works on macOS and is used to copy data to the clipboard. On other operating systems, the command may differ and you may need to use **xclip** or **xsel** to copy the key to the clipboard.

I love that ChatGPT goes above and beyond the actual command, providing examples, options, and even caveats.

Commands Specific to macOS

So far, I've been impressed with what both Copilot and ChatGPT were able to do. There are other commands that I have a hard time remembering, particularly commands on macOS that manipulate media files. Let's see how they did with some of those.

Unfortunately, I seem to have hit the limit of Copilot's abilities. Each of the comments I tried did not result in working commands. Here is the first, asking Copilot to convert a folder of JPEG files to PNG format.

The command it gave me doesn't work on my Mac, but it looks like it should.

```
# Convert all jpg files in the current directory to png files
for file in *.jpg; do
    convert "$file" "${file%.jpg}.png"
done
```

ChatGPT, naturally, explained why.

> *Convert all jpg files in the current directory to png files*
>
> You can use the command-line tool **convert** from ImageMagick to convert all JPG files in the current directory to PNG files. Here is an example of how to use **convert** to convert all JPG files to PNG files:
>
> ```
> for file in *.jpg; do convert "$file" "${file%.jpg}.png"; done
> ```
>
> This command will loop through all files in the current directory that have a **.jpg** extension, run the **convert** command on each file, and save the output to a new file with the same name but with a **.png** extension.
>
> Alternatively, you can use **find** and **mogrify** command from ImageMagick:
>
> ```
> find . -name "*.jpg" -exec mogrify -format png {} +
> ```
>
> This command will search for all **.jpg** files in the current directory and its subdirectories and change their format to **.png** and overwrite the original files.
>
> Please note that this will overwrite the original JPG files. If you want to keep the original files, you can modify the command to save the output to a different location or with a different file name.

Interestingly, its first suggestion matched Copilot's identically. The difference is that ChatGPT told me that the convert command comes from ImageMagick. Deciding not to give up just yet, I asked it how to install ImageMagick.

This is what it told me.

> *How do I install ImageMagick?*
>
> To install ImageMagick on macOS, you can use the package manager Homebrew. Here are the steps to install ImageMagick using Homebrew:
>
> Install Homebrew if you haven't already by running the following command in the terminal:

```
/bin/bash   -c   "$(curl   -fsSL   https://raw.githubusercontent.com/Homebrew/install/HEAD/
install.sh)"
```

Once Homebrew is installed, you can use it to install ImageMagick by running the following command in the terminal:

```
brew install imagemagick
```

After the installation is complete, you can check that it was successful by running the following command:

```
convert -version
```

This will display the version of ImageMagick that you have installed.

Another way to install ImageMagick on macOS is to download the binary package from the official website and install it manually. You can find the binary package here: https://imagemagick.org/script/download.php#macosx

Please note that you may need to add the ImageMagick binaries to your system's PATH for the **convert** and **mogrify** command to be recognized by the terminal.

I had similar issues with other commands. This one also didn't work for me, but there was no hint as to what the error might be.

```
# Extract audio from all the mp4 files in the folder
for file in *.mp4; do
    ffmpeg -i "$file" -vn -acodec copy "${file%.mp4}.mp3"
done
```

As expected, ChatGPT gave me a lot more context, after suggesting a very similar command, but also explaining what I needed to understand about it.

Extract audio from all the mp4 files in the folder

You can use the command-line tool **ffmpeg** to extract the audio from all MP4 files in a folder on macOS. Here is an example of how to use **ffmpeg** to extract the audio from all MP4 files in the current directory and save it as an MP3 file:

```
for file in *.mp4; do ffmpeg -i "$file" -vn -acodec libmp3lame -ac 2 -q:a 4 -y "${file%.mp4}.mp3"; done
```

This command will loop through all files in the current directory that have a **.mp4** extension, run the **ffmpeg** command on each file, and save the audio output to a new file with the same name but with a **.mp3** extension.

This command uses the -i option to specify the input file, the -vn option to disable the video stream, the -acodec option to specify the audio codec, -ac 2 to specify the number of audio channels, -q:a 4 to specify the audio quality and -y to overwriting output files.

You can change the output file format and codec by changing the **mp3** and **libmp3lame** accordingly.

Please note that you may need to install **ffmpeg** in your system if it is not already installed. You can install **ffmpeg** using Homebrew by running the following command in the terminal:

```
brew install ffmpeg
```

Also, please note that this command will overwrite any existing files with the same name. If you want to keep the original files, you can modify the command to save the output to a different location or with a different file name.

The command ChatGPT gave me was more complete, but its explanation is misleading. Or maybe I simply read it wrong. The `-y` parameter will automatically overwrite any existing files on output, but the command is not destructive to the input files.

My final test was to try to extract audio using `avconvert`, another command on macOS. Copilot gave me a single command.

```
# Extract audio from video file using avconvert
avconvert -i video.mp4 -vn -acodec copy audio.mp3
```

Apparently, this command no longer exists, which ChatGPT was happy to explain to me when I asked about it.

What is avconvert?

avconv is a command-line tool similar to **ffmpeg** that can be used to convert multimedia files. To extract the audio from a video file using **avconv** on macOS, you can use the following command:

```
avconv -i inputfile.mp4 -vn -acodec libmp3lame -ac 2 -q:a 4 -y outputfile.mp3
```

This command uses the **-i** option to specify the input file, the **-vn** option to disable the video stream, the **-acodec** option to specify the audio codec as **libmp3lame**, the **-ac 2** option to specify the number of audio channels, the **-q:a 4** option to specify the audio quality and the **-y** option to overwrite output files if they already exist.

You can change the input and output file name and format accordingly, also you can change the codec and quality options as you need.

Please note that you may need to install **avconv** in your system if it is not already installed. You can install **avconv** using Homebrew by running the following command in the terminal:

```
brew install libav
```

> Please note that **avconv** and **ffmpeg** are similar but not exactly the same, and their syntax and options may differ slightly. Some options or codecs that work with **ffmpeg** may not work with **avconv**, and vice versa. Also, **ffmpeg** is more commonly used and has more active development than **avconv**, but both of them can be used to extract audio from a video file.

Note that it didn't answer the question that I asked, or so I thought. Confused and mildly curious, I then asked for clarification.

> *What is the difference between avconv and avconvert?*
>
> **avconv** and **avconvert** are actually the same thing, **avconv** is the command-line tool for the **libav** library, that is a fork of the **ffmpeg** library. **avconv** was the command-line tool for the **libav** library and it's the equivalent of the **ffmpeg** command-line tool for the **ffmpeg** library, but the **libav** project was discontinued in 2018 and now the **libav** developers recommend using **ffmpeg** instead of **avconv**. **avconvert** is a typo or a misspelling of **avconv**, and both commands can be used to perform the same tasks. The **avconv** tool has been replaced by **ffmpeg**, but you might find some old resources or scripts that use **avconv** or **avconvert**.
>
> In summary, **avconv** and **avconvert** are the same command-line tool, but the **libav** project was discontinued in 2018 and now it's recommended to use **ffmpeg** instead of **avconv**.

I got none of that context from Copilot. What amazed me is that I thought `avconvert` was the current and correct command to use. Apparently, I was mistaken on both counts.

Parting Thoughts

While using AI tools can potentially save time and effort, it is important to assess the quality of the generated commands and ensure they are safe and effective. The output from ChatGPT is superior to that of Copilot, but I expected that for the purposes of this chapter.

ChatGPT is an advanced AI model that is capable of understanding and responding to more complex and nuanced questions. Copilot is an AI assistant designed to help developers with their coding tasks, but it's not as advanced as ChatGPT. However, the important thing here is that either one can help you accomplish your task effectively. Both ChatGPT and Copilot can provide accurate and reliable answers to your questions, but ChatGPT's output is more detailed and comprehensive. Ultimately, the choice of which tool to use will depend on your specific needs and preferences.

In addition to the difference in output quality, another aspect to consider is the area of expertise of each tool. ChatGPT is a general-purpose language model that has been trained on a vast amount of text data, making it a good choice when the subject matter may be unfamiliar, or when you need an explanation or clarification. It is good at providing a comprehensive understanding of a topic, and it can be used for a wide range of tasks, including language translation, text generation, and question answering.

On the other hand, Copilot is an AI assistant that is specifically designed for developers and is trained on actual software. Therefore, may be better at understanding your code in context and providing solutions that are tailored to your specific needs.

As you will continue to see, it can help you with your coding tasks by suggesting snippets of code, providing documentation, and even completing your code for you.

If you are a developer and you need help with your code, Copilot is a great choice.

GIT COMMANDS

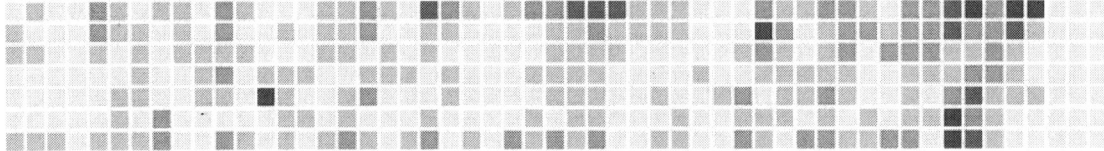

GitHub Commit Graph by Author

Can GitHub Copilot Help with Git Itself?

After my experience with shell scripting, I decided to explore how Copilot could assist with learning Git commands. In this chapter, I will detail my findings and demonstrate how Copilot can effectively aid in the learning process.

Basic Git Commands

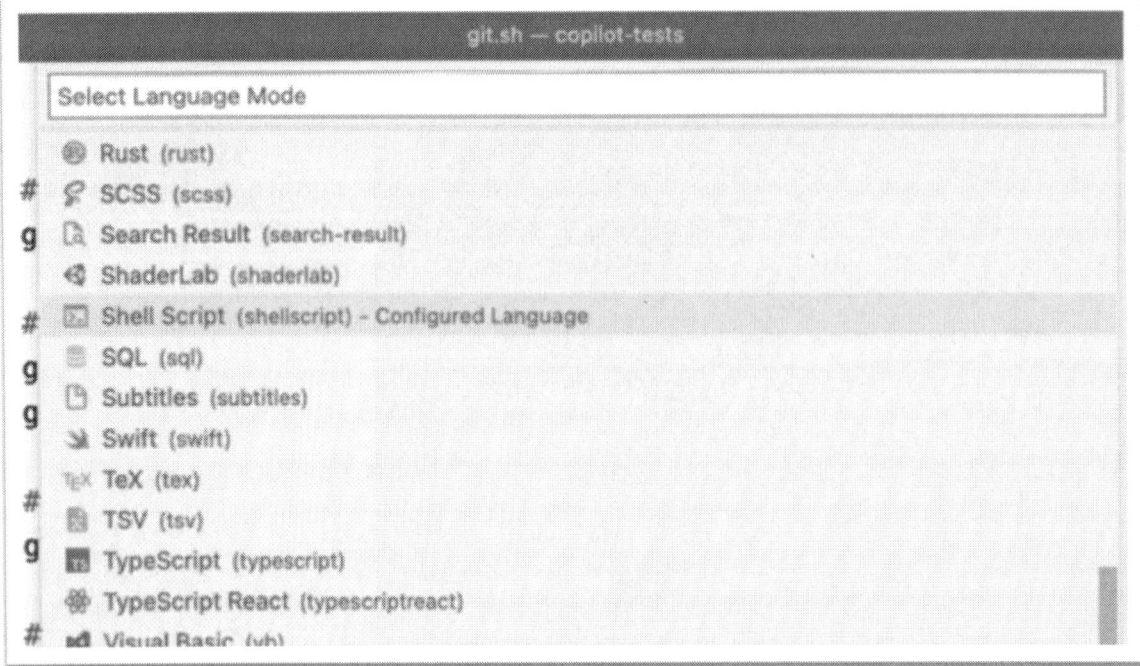

As I did with shell scripting, I created a blank document in VS Code and set its type to Shell Script. Next, I started adding comments into the document to see what Copilot would suggest. In every case you see below, I typed as little as possible to exercise Copilot to its fullest.

I started simple, just asking it to create a new git repository for me.

```shell
# Create an empty git repo
git init
```

Next, I wanted to set my git name and email, but I can never remember the exact commands. Copilot, however, does.

```shell
# Set my git user name and email
git config user.name "Mike Callaghan"
git config user.email "michael@walkingriver.com"
```

Sadly, but understandably, Copilot didn't know my name and email address. I added those myself. It suggested "John Doe," which was an easy hint that I would have to change it. For the email, it stopped the suggested text at the opening quote, suggesting that I complete the line myself.

An empty git repo isn't very useful, so I wanted to create a new branch, add a file to it, and then commit the changes and push the branch. Here are those commands, all as suggested by Copilot from my comments:

```shell
# Create and switch to a new branch named develop
git checkout -b develop
# Create a file
echo "Hello World" > hello.txt
# Commit all new and updated files to this branch
git add .
git commit -m "Initial commit"
# Push this branch to the remote repository
git push -u origin develop
```

```
# Switch back to the main branch
git checkout main
# Merge the develop branch into the main branch
git merge develop
# Rebase the main branch onto the develop branch
git checkout develop
git rebase main
```

Those are all pretty good guesses. So far, I'm pleased with how well Copilot understands git.

Intermediate Git Commands

For the rest of the chapter, I ran the generated commands on a mature repo, rather than the one I created above. This one has multiple branches, commits, tags, etc.

Commit Logs

Git-log enables you to view a quick summary of a repo's commits in reverse order, newest to oldest. Copilot helped me learn a number of variations on that command.

```
# Show me the last 10 commits on develop branch
git log --oneline -10 develop
# Show me the last 10 commits on all branches
git log --oneline -10 --all
# Show me the last 10 commits on all branches and show the graph
git log --oneline -10 --all --graph
# Show me the last 10 commits on all branches and show the graph and author
git log --oneline -10 --all --graph --author="Mike Callaghan"
```

I'm not sure this one is accurate. I believe that it will show me all commits by Mike Callaghan, but necessary all commits and their authors. Again, be careful with simply accepting what Copilot provides at face value. It can help, but if you are careless, it can also hurt you.

Revert Mistaken Commits

I have a hard time remembering the correct git commands to revert changes I didn't mean to commit. Would Copilot allow me to stop referring to that article? Here is what it gave me when I asked.

```
# Revert last commit
git reset --hard HEAD~1
# Revert last commit and keep changes
git reset --soft HEAD~1
# Revert all commits from ee670f5 to 9ad6740
git revert ee670f5..9ad6740
```

Those are exactly correct.

Cherry Pick

Sometimes we want to select a single prior commit from another branch and apply it to the current branch. This is called cherry picking, and Copilot knew how to do that, too.

```
# Cherry pick commit 9ad6740 into main
git checkout main
git cherry-pick 9ad6740
```

Git Diff

If you want to view what has changed between two commits, you use the git-diff command.

```
# Compare commits ee670f5 with 9ad6740
git diff ee670f5 9ad6740
```

This works, but it isn't very intuitive. Maybe there is a better option?

DiffMerge

There is an app I've used before called DiffMerge that gives you a nicer UI for comparing diffs. I wondered whether Copilot could help me install and configure it.

```
# install diffmerge from brew
```

```
brew install --cask diffmerge
# Set the difftool to diffmerge
git config --global diff.tool diffmerge
git config --global difftool.diffmerge.cmd 'diffmerge "$LOCAL" "$REMOTE"'
git config --global difftool.prompt false
# Compare commits ee670f5 with 9ad6740 with an external diff tool
git difftool ee670f5 9ad6740
```

Note that even though DiffMerge runs on both macOS and Windows, the `brew` command is specific to macOS. I asked it to install on Windows instead and it gave me this:

```
# install diffmerge on windows
choco install diffmerge
```

I don't have a Windows box to try it, but it looks legitimate. The rest of the commands above should be the same.

Advanced Git Commands

I don't profess to be a git expert. I consider myself an intermediate student at best. That said, I have done a few more advanced activities with git, and I present them here for your edification.

Archive Repo

Have you ever needed to send someone a copy of your git repo without any of the git stuff attached? You could checkout the correct branch at the desired commit, remove the `.git` folder, and then zip it up. Did you know that git can do all that for you?

```
# Archive the current branch
git archive -o archive.zip HEAD
# Archive the current branch and exclude the .gitignore files
git archive -o archive.zip HEAD -- . ':!*.gitignore'
# Archive commit 1319f65 and exclude the .gitignore files
git archive -o archive.zip 1319f65 -- . ':!*.gitignore'
```

Clean up Stale Branches and Files

After a pull request is completed, it's often a good idea to clean up older feature branches. GitHub and GitLab can be configured to do this automatically. The trouble is, doing so on your local repo isn't so easy.

```
# Remove all merged branches
git branch --merged | grep -v "\*" | xargs -n 1 git branch -d
```

Sometimes, you may want to delete an individual branch that exists on both your local repo and the remote.

```
# Delete myfeature branch on local and remote
git branch -d myfeature
git push origin --delete myfeature
```

What if you have untracked files on your local, and want to clean them up?

```
# Delete untracked local files from the current working tree
git clean -f
```

Shallow Clones

Have you ever had a git repository grow so large that it took up way too much disk space? After a while, you might decide that you don't need the full history, and it would be easier to clone only a portion of it. This is called a "shallow clone," and Copilot knows how to do it.

```
# Clone repo keeping only commits after Jan 1, 2022
git clone --shallow-since=2022-01-01

# Clone repo keeping only commits after Jan 1, 2022 and before Jan 1, 2023
git clone --shallow-since=2022-01-01 --shallow-until=2023-01-01

# Clone repo keeping only commits after Jan 1, 2022 and before Jan 1, 2023 and only the main branch
git clone --shallow-since=2022-01-01 --shallow-until=2023-01-01 --branch main

# Clone repo keeping only commits after Jan 1, 2022 and before Jan 1, 2023 and only the main branch and only the last 10 commits
git clone --shallow-since=2022-01-01 --shallow-until=2023-01-01 --branch main --depth 10
```

At this point, I don't feel it's necessary for me to try to remember these commands. Copilot will remember them for me.

Permanently Remove a File

For my last operation, imagine you have accidentally committed a file containing secrets (passwords, private keys, etc.) to your remote repo. If you simply delete it from your local, add the file to `.gitignore`, and commit, that won't do the trick. The file can still be restored. The only way to remove a file in this manner is to rewrite history. Fortunately, git can do this, but it's easier said than done, as you'll see.

This is what Copilot offered when I asked it to delete a file of secrets.

```
# Delete secrets file accidentally committed to git
git filter-branch --force --index-filter 'git rm --cached --ignore-unmatch secrets.txt' --prune-empty --tag-name-filter cat -- --all
```

To be honest, I didn't want to test this command, but I decided to give it a try on an unimportant repo. I switched out `secrets.txt` with `package-lock.json`, figuring it wouldn't be terribly dangerous to remove that particular file.

When I ran it, git gave me a large warning:

```
git-filter-branch has a glut of gotchas generating mangled history
rewrites.  Hit Ctrl-C before proceeding to abort, then use an
alternative filtering tool such as 'git filter-repo'
(https://github.com/newren/git-filter-repo/) instead.  See the
filter-branch manual page for more details; to squelch this warning,
set FILTER_BRANCH_SQUELCH_WARNING=1.
```

I let it run, figuring "what's the worst that can happen?" What happened is that it removed every instance of `package-lock.json` in my entire project. Beyond that, the local and remote repos diverged by 20-some commits, so I never did figure out if that's what I wanted.

I asked Copilot to fix my diverged branches, and it offered this:

```
# Fix diverged branches
git fetch --all
git reset --hard origin/main
```

It worked, and now I'm back to where I was when I started.

Now, what was that warning all about? Maybe it's something we should consider. I looked into `git-filter-repo`, and it looks like a better solution. Also, as it turned out, Copilot seemed to know about that, too.

```
# Delete secrets file accidentally pushed to remote with filter-repo
git filter-repo --path-glob '!secrets.txt'
```

As I didn't have it installed, the command didn't work. However, I was impressed that it came up with the correct syntax (I presume).

Final Words

With the exception of the last request and that one tiny issue with `git log`, Copilot handled everything I threw at it. I'll probably keep using it whenever I can't remember exactly which git command to use.

You may be wondering why I didn't use ChatGPT here. I expect that it would be able to get these same commands correct. I urge you to give it a shot as an exercise. Drop me an email and let me know how it goes.

COMMON ALGORITHMS

Image by Markus Spiske from Pixabay

One of my favorite uses for AI is to have it generate code for common algorithms. In this chapter, I will highlight some real-world situations where I have used it to solve common problems.

IIFE

Do you know what an IIFE is in JavaScript? Well, just ask ChatGPT!

> What's an IIFE in Javascript, why would I need one, and how would I create one?

IIFE stands for Immediately Invoked Function Expression. It is a common design pattern used in

JavaScript to create a private scope for your code and avoid polluting the global namespace with variables and functions.

You might use an IIFE in situations where you need to encapsulate some code and prevent it from affecting other code on the page. For example, you might use an IIFE to define a module in your application, where the module's code is contained within the IIFE's private scope.

To create an IIFE, you simply define a function expression and wrap it in parentheses to make it an expression. You can then immediately invoke the function by appending a pair of parentheses after it, like this:

```
(function() {
  // your code here
})();
```

In this example, an anonymous function is defined and immediately invoked. The function creates a private scope for the code inside it, preventing any variables or functions declared within it from leaking into the global scope.

Note that the parentheses around the function expression are necessary, because they cause the function to be interpreted as an expression rather than a declaration. Without these parentheses, the JavaScript parser would interpret the function as a function declaration, which can only be used in certain contexts.

That's a pretty impressive explanation. It actually gave me a longer explanation, but I pared it down for you.

Granted, with TypeScript, we hardly need to use IIFEs anymore. In fact, what if we asked ChatGPT to convert its last IIFE into an equivalent TypeScript class?

What would be the equivalent of that code if we were to use classes in TypeScript instead?

If you were to use classes in TypeScript to achieve a similar result as the IIFE example, you could define a class and use the **constructor** method to execute your code.

Here's an example:

```
class MyClass {
  constructor() {
    // your code here
  }
}
```

```
new MyClass();
```

In this example, the **MyClass** constructor function is executed immediately when an instance of the class is created using the **new** keyword.

You could also pass arguments to the constructor method, like this:

```
class MyClass {
  constructor(arg1, arg2) {
    // your code here
  }
}
new MyClass(val1, val2);
```

In this case, the arguments **val1** and **val2** are passed to the constructor method as **arg1** and **arg2**, respectively.

Using classes in TypeScript provides additional benefits, such as better type checking and encapsulation, as well as the ability to define public and private members. However, the overall goal of both the IIFE and class examples is the same: to encapsulate your code and prevent it from affecting other code on the page.

Notice I didn't have to restate my request, but simply asked it to rewrite "that code." This is our first example of ChatGPT remembering the context of the conversation.

Array Functions

Copilot and ChatGPT are really good at helping manipulate arrays. All you need to do is ask.

Reduce

For some reason, I can never remember how to use JavaScript's `reduce` function to calculate the sum of the items in an array. GitHub Copilot knew, however. I simply provided a comment of what I wanted to accomplish, and let Copilot do the rest.

Consider the following array of "puzzles." This is a I snippet from my game Foreword, a game of word squares.

```
// Partial array of "puzzles" for this example
private demoPuzzles: Puzzle[] = [
```

```
  { id:88, size: 4, solution: ['abetbabeebontent'] },
  { id:89, size: 4, solution: ['icedcaveevendent'] },
  { id:90, size: 8, solution: ['abetracemirestun', 'armsbaitecruteen'] },
  { id:91, size: 8, solution: ['cageheaturicmyth', 'chumaerygaitetch'] }
];
```

Notice that some puzzles have one solution, and some have two. My actual array of puzzles has thousands of elements.

Now let's assume I want to count the total number of solutions in my puzzle array. I provided Copilot with a simple comment and let it generate the code.

```
// Count the total number of solutions in the demo Puzzle array
const total = this.demoPuzzles.reduce((acc, puzzle) => acc + puzzle.solution.length, 0);
```

Yeah, I could have used a `for` loop, or looked up the syntax of `Array.reduce`, but Copilot did this for me, with nothing more than a comment. To me, that's productive!

Filter

Next, imagine I want to find all the puzzles in the array of size 4. I gave Copilot the first comment. It then proceeded to write the second comment.

```
// Find all puzzles with a size of 4
// Find all puzzles with a size of 8
```

It was able to do this because it knows the context of the application and can see what else I'm doing. By recognizing some of the puzzles were size 4 and some size 8, it offered the second comment. What happened next surprised me. Instead of giving me the array filter function I was expecting, it gave me this.

```
public findPuzzlesBySize(size: number): Puzzle[] {
  return this.demoPuzzles.filter(puzzle => puzzle.size === size);
}
```

That's right. It gave me a generic function to find puzzles by any size.

When I gave the same prompt to ChatGPT, it went in a slightly different direction.

Given an array that looks like the following array, find all puzzles of size 4 or 8. (I then pasted the puzzles

> *array).*
>
> To find all puzzles of size 4 or 8, you can use the **filter** method on the **demoPuzzles** array and provide a callback function that checks the size of each puzzle:
>
> ```
> const filteredPuzzles = demoPuzzles.filter(puzzle => puzzle.size === 4 || puzzle.size === 8);
> ```
>
> This will return a new array that contains only the puzzles that have a size of 4 or 8.
>
> You could also use the forEach method and check the size of each puzzle, then push the matching puzzles into a new array:
>
> ```
> const filteredPuzzles = [];
> demoPuzzles.forEach(puzzle => {
>   if (puzzle.size === 4 || puzzle.size === 8) {
>     filteredPuzzles.push(puzzle);
>   }
> });
> ```
>
> This achieves the same result as the **filter** method.
>
> In either case, the resulting **filteredPuzzles** array will contain only the puzzles of size 4 or 8.

In this case, ChatGPT took me literally, giving me a way to find puzzles of either size 4 or of size 8. The odd thing is that the code it gave me will produce an array with the identical contents as the original, which is not at all helpful.

Copilot, on the other hand, gave me code that was closer to what I needed. Consider that a win for Copilot.

Sort

What if I wanted to sort the array? I know that JavaScript has a `sort` function and that it takes a call-back function that describes how the sort should be done. But maybe I can't quite remember the syntax.

Asking Copilot to sort my array of puzzles with the larger (size 8) puzzles at the beginning, gave me this:

```
// Sort the puzzles by size, with the largest first
puzzles = this.demoPuzzles.sort((a, b) => b.size - a.size);
```

Notice that this time, Copilot simply gave me a one-liner instead of a complete function. In my experience, this is more consistent with how Copilot usually responds.

ChatGPT offered me this response.

> const sortedPuzzles = demoPuzzles.sort((a, b) => b.size - a.size);
>
> This will return a new array that contains the puzzles sorted by size, with the largest first.
>
> In this example, the **sort** method takes a callback function that compares the **size** property of the **a** and **b** objects. By subtracting **a.size** from **b.size**, we ensure that the puzzles are sorted in descending order based on size.

The two functions are identical, which is good sign. I still love that ChatGPT offers an explanation for its suggestions, whereas Copilot assumes you only need it to write the code.

Array as a Stack or a Queue

Sometimes we want to implement a stack or a queue with arrays. Copilot and ChatGPT can help with that also.

ChatGPT gave me a complete set of strongly typed TypeScript functions when I asked it to do so:

```
Generate a set of strongly typed TypeScript functions to treat the array like a stack or queue.

type Puzzle = { id: number; size: number; solution: string[] };

function pushToStack(stack: Puzzle[], puzzle: Puzzle): Puzzle[] {
  return [...stack, puzzle];
}

function popFromStack(stack: Puzzle[]): [Puzzle | undefined, Puzzle[]] {
  const poppedPuzzle = stack[stack.length - 1];
  const newStack = stack.slice(0, stack.length - 1);
  return [poppedPuzzle, newStack];
}

function enqueue(queue: Puzzle[], puzzle: Puzzle): Puzzle[] {
```

```
  return [...queue, puzzle];
}
function dequeue(queue: Puzzle[]): [Puzzle | undefined, Puzzle[]] {
  const dequeuedPuzzle = queue[0];
  const newQueue = queue.slice(1);
  return [dequeuedPuzzle, newQueue];
}
```

As usual, it provided a complete explanation for each function.

Copilot was far more concise, though it wrote every line after my first comment (including the new comments).

```
// Function to add a new puzzle to the list of puzzles like a queue
addPuzzle() {
  this.demoPuzzles.push({ id: 92, size: 4, solution: ['cageheaturicmyth', 'chumaerygaitetch'] });
}
// Function to remove a puzzle from the list of puzzles like a queue
removePuzzle() {
  this.demoPuzzles.pop();
}
// Function to add a new puzzle to the list of puzzles like a stack
pushPuzzle() {
  this.demoPuzzles.unshift({ id: 92, size: 4, solution: ['cageheaturicmyth', 'chumaerygaitetch'] });
}
// Function to remove a puzzle from the list of puzzles like a stack
popPuzzle() {
  this.demoPuzzles.shift();
}
```

Notice that it did not try to create a new `Puzzle` type for me. It knew I already had data and only gave me what I needed in context of my application.

What it got totally wrong, however, was assuming I wanted a hard-coded puzzle literal (and an invalid one at that) instead of giving the function a `Puzzle` parameter.

Fortunately, all Copilot needs to fix that incorrect assumption is a reworded comment.

```
// Function to add a new puzzle to the list of puzzles like a queue,
// which takes a strongly typed Puzzle object as a parameter
addPuzzle(puzzle: Puzzle) {
  this.demoPuzzles.push(puzzle);
}
```

It got the rest of the functions right, but for this example, I didn't think I needed to show all the code again.

Array to Hash

In one of my projects, I queried a remote web service to retrieve customer and sales information, which was returned in data structure that looked something like the following.

```
"orders": [
  {
    "id": "order1",
    "customerName": "John Smith",
    "productName": "Shirt",
    "quantity": 2,
    "price": 25
  },
  {
    "id": "order2",
```

```
    "customerName": "Jane Doe",
    "productName": "Pants",
    "quantity": 1,
    "price": 40
  },
  {
    "id": "order3",
    "customerName": "Bob Johnson",
    "productName": "Socks",
    "quantity": 3,
    "price": 10
  }
]
```

Notice that `orders` is an array, with each order being a self-contained object in the array. Now imagine that there are hundreds or thousands of such orders. If I wanted to grab just `order72`, I would have to traverse the entire array. If the data structure were a hash instead, with each order having its `id` as the key, it would be much simpler (and faster) to get any arbitrary element.

I could very quickly come up with code that loops through the entire array and generates a new hash object, but this is the sort of mundane task at which ChatGPT excels. This is the prompt I gave it, followed by the code it produced.

ChatGPT offered to use the `reduce` function, which honestly never occurred to me. As I told you before, it's not a function that I'm good at. It's one of my (many?) blind spots.

> *I have an array in TypeScript with the following shape. (I pasted the above JSON here). I want to convert it from an array to a hash array so that can address each object by its "id".*
>
> You can convert the array to a hash array by using the **reduce** method and creating a new object with the "id" property as the key. Here's an example:
>
> ```
> const hashArray = orders.reduce((acc, config) => {
>   acc[config.id] = config;
> ```

```
    return acc;
}, {});
```
Now you can access each object by its "id" like this: **hashArray["order2"]**.

I then further refined it by asking for a standalone function, which it created for me (not shown).

String Manipulation

Do you find yourself manipulating text often? I know I do. Extracting smaller bits of text from long inputs, determining whether one string exists inside another, dealing with padding, etc. Those sorts of things are reasonably straightforward, but I prefer not to type this stuff if I don't have to.

String searches

Consider the problem of finding every occurrence of a word inside a longer string. How would ChatGPT approach it?

```
const text = "The quick brown fox jumps over the lazy dog.";
// Find all occurrences of the substring "the" (case-insensitive)
const substring = /the/gi;
const matches = text.match(substring);
// Print the matches
console.log(matches);
```

ChatGPT went directly to regular expressions. I'll dive deeper into regexes later in the book.

Copilot also used a regular expression, but it went in an entirely different direction.

```
const regex = /the/gi;
let m;
while ((m = regex.exec(text)) !== null) {
  // This is necessary to avoid infinite loops with zero-width matches
  if (m.index === regex.lastIndex) {
```

```
  regex.lastIndex++;
}
// The result can be accessed through the `m`-variable.
m.forEach((match, groupIndex) => {
  console.log(`Found match, group ${groupIndex}: ${match}`);
});
}
```

In all honesty, I'm not entirely sure I understand what Copilot gave me there. For fun, I pasted Copilot's code sample into ChatGPT and asked it to explain it to me. This is what it said.

> This JavaScript code finds all occurrences of the substring "the" in a given piece of text using regular expressions, and logs the matches to the console. Here's a breakdown of how it works:
>
> const regex = /the/gi; - This line creates a regular expression regex that matches the substring "the" with the /the/ syntax. The g and i flags are used to perform a global search and a case-insensitive search, respectively.
>
> let m; - This line declares a variable m without initializing it.
>
> while ((m = regex.exec(text)) !== null) { - This line sets m to the result of calling the regex.exec(text) method, which returns an array of information about the next match of the regular expression in the text string. The while loop continues as long as m is not null.
>
> if (m.index === regex.lastIndex) { regex.lastIndex++; } - This line checks whether the match is a zero-width match (i.e., an empty string), and if so, increments the lastIndex property of the regex object to avoid an infinite loop.
>
> m.forEach((match, groupIndex) => { console.log(Found match, group ${groupIndex}: ${match}); }); - This line loops through each match in the m array using the forEach() method, and logs each match and its group index to the console using a template literal.
>
> Overall, this code is a more advanced version of the previous code examples, using the regex.exec() method to iterate over each match and access its properties. The use of forEach() allows for more fine-grained control over the output and provides access to the match's group index, which can be useful when working with more complex regular expressions.

Do you see what it did? Read that final paragraph carefully. ChatGPT recognized that the code I pasted from Copilot was related to my original question, and then explained that it was a more advanced example of the same concept. Truly amazing!

Removing whitespace

Sometimes, you may be faced with a lengthy piece of text with too much whitespace. Given such a string, how would you remove its excess whitespace, while preserving the important text?

For this example, I asked ChatGPT to generate some sample "lorem ipsum" text with lots of extra whitespace.

```
const loremIpsumWithWhitespace = `

Lorem ipsum    dolor sit amet, consectetur adipiscing elit. Fusce molestie turpis   nec   felis malesuada accumsan. Vestibulum   tincidunt lacus nec nulla dignissim blandit. Morbi tristique, enim eu imperdiet luctus, nisl turpis aliquam nunc, eu interdum purus velit  quis velit.  Curabitur vel semper tellus,  at iaculis lectus. Morbi sed lectus  ac nibh eleifend tristique. Praesent sagittis elit vel dui consequat,  eu maximus purus molestie. Integer varius  pharetra odio, non vestibulum urna lobortis et.  Sed et eleifend lorem, quis mollis ipsum.

Pellentesque     consectetur   mauris sed risus laoreet,   vel malesuada augue convallis.   Nullam vestibulum  commodo metus, id tristique est suscipit id. Etiam  pretium  sagittis malesuada. Vivamus sit amet mi lorem.  Etiam hendrerit euismod libero, nec   accumsan massa laoreet vel. Donec  viverra felis et urna fringilla, non convallis tellus egestas. Suspendisse faucibus quam in erat sagittis  dignissim. Duis maximus risus sit amet eros bibendum feugiat. `;
```

Next, I asked for a generic function that would accept that type of input and return the string with all the insignificant whitespace removed.

```
function removeInsignificantWhitespace(text) {
  // Replace all whitespace characters with a single space
  const stripped = text.replace(/\s+/g, " ");
  // Remove leading/trailing spaces and line breaks
  return stripped.trim();
}
```

This function works by first using a regular expression (**/\s+/g**) to match all occurrences of one or more whitespace characters (spaces, tabs, line breaks, etc.) and replacing them with a single space character using the **replace()** method.

The resulting string is then passed to the **trim()** method, which removes any leading or trailing spaces or line breaks.

> This ensures that the final output contains only the necessary whitespace characters (e.g., spaces between words) and no unnecessary ones.

For Copilot's test, I started with the long JavaScript constant from before and gave it a similar prompt. Its result was a little terser.

```
// Function to remove all the whitespace from a string
function removeWhitespace(text: string) {
  return text.replace(/\s/g, '');
}
```

What's amusing about Copilot's result is that it suggested its own comment after I pasted in the lengthy text. Always remember that Copilot's strength is in its awareness of your entire application.

Whitespace Padding

Now, let's consider the puzzle array. If I wanted to generate some pretty formatting using only text in a fixed-width font, how might I do that? ChatGPT gave me the following function, along with a sample of what the output would look like:

```
const printTable = (puzzles: Puzzle[]): void => {
  console.log('ID  Size  Solution');
  console.log('--------------------');
  puzzles.forEach(puzzle => {
      console.log(`${puzzle.id.toString().padEnd(4, ' ')}${puzzle.size.toString().padEnd(6, ' ')}${puzzle.solution[0]}`);
  });
};
printTable(demoPuzzles);
```

> This code will output the **demoPuzzles** array as a table with fixed-width font, like this:
>
> ID Size Solution
>
> --------------------
>
> 88 4   abetbabeebontent

```
89  4  icedcaveevendent
90  8  abetracemirestun
91  8  cageheaturicmyth
```

Copilot gave me something different, but I think in this case it cheated.

```
// Print the puzzles array as a table, using only text, suitable for output with a fixed-width font.
printPuzzles() {
  let puzzleTable = this.demoPuzzles.map(p => {
    return { id: p.id, size: p.size, solution: p.solution.join(' ') };
  });
  console.table(puzzleTable);
}
```

Technically, `console.table` will do exactly what I asked, so in that respect was correct. I decided to give it another hint to see if I could get it to write something closer to what ChatGPT did.

```
// Print the puzzles array as a table, using only text, suitable for output with a fixed-width font, using console.log.
printPuzzles() {
  // Get the longest puzzle id, so we can pad the id column to align the puzzle data.
  const longestId = this.demoPuzzles.reduce((longest, puzzle) => Math.max(longest, puzzle.id.toString().length), 0);
  // Print the header row.
  console.log(`id${' '.repeat(longestId - 2)} | size | solution`);
  console.log('-'.repeat(longestId + 2) + '-+-' + '-'.repeat(5) + '-+-' + '-'.repeat(16));
  // Print the puzzle rows.
  this.demoPuzzles.forEach(puzzle => {
    console.log(`${puzzle.id}${' '.repeat(longestId - puzzle.id.toString().length)} | ${puzzle.size} | ${puzzle.solution.join(' ')}`);
```

```
    });
}
```

It did a better job on the second pass. What do you think? I like the fact that it looks for the longest id so that I can pad the columns correctly. That was a nice touch.

Generating CSV Files

What if I wanted to output the array as a comma-separated file instead? Copilot gave me almost the same code as above, but with some extra logic.

```
// Generate a CSV file containing the puzzles array
generateCsv() {
    // Create a CSV file, with a header row, and a row for each puzzle.
    const csv = 'id,size,solution\r\n' + this.demoPuzzles.map(puzzle => `${puzzle.id},${puzzle.size},"${puzzle.solution.join(' ')}"`).join('\r\n');
    // Write the CSV file to disk.
    require('fs').writeFileSync('puzzles.csv', csv);
}
```

One of the dangers in relying on an AI to do the work for you is that it might create buggy code that looks reasonable. In this case, if any of my fields contained commas, the output generated by this function would most likely be unreadable as a CSV file.

ChatGPT gave me almost the same code, except that it accounted for potential commas in my puzzle fields.

```
import * as fs from 'fs';
const generateCSV = (puzzles: Puzzle[]): void => {
    const header = 'id,size,solution\n';
    const rows = puzzles.map(puzzle => `${puzzle.id},${puzzle.size},"${puzzle.solution.join(';')}"\n`);
    const csv = header + rows.join('');
    fs.writeFileSync('puzzles.csv', csv);
};
```

```
generateCSV(demoPuzzles);
```

Notice that both solutions assumed I'm using Node, in that each solution uses the `fs` library. ChatGPT took extra care to inform me that I would need the `fs` module from NodeJS.

> Note that in order to run this code, you will need to have the **fs** module and the Node.js runtime installed.

Generate HTML

I could also ask it to generate HTML for me. ChatGPT did exactly what I asked it to, again remembering the shape of my puzzles array and objects.

```
Create a function in JavaScript that will output the puzzles array as an HTML table

function printTable(puzzles) {
  const table = document.createElement('table');
  const headerRow = document.createElement('tr');
  const idHeader = document.createElement('th');
  const sizeHeader = document.createElement('th');
  const solutionHeader = document.createElement('th');
  idHeader.textContent = 'ID';
  sizeHeader.textContent = 'Size';
  solutionHeader.textContent = 'Solution';
  headerRow.appendChild(idHeader);
  headerRow.appendChild(sizeHeader);
  headerRow.appendChild(solutionHeader);
  table.appendChild(headerRow);
  puzzles.forEach(puzzle => {
    const row = document.createElement('tr');
    const idCell = document.createElement('td');
    const sizeCell = document.createElement('td');
```

```
  const solutionCell = document.createElement('td');

  idCell.textContent = puzzle.id;

  sizeCell.textContent = puzzle.size;

  solutionCell.textContent = puzzle.solution.join(';');

  row.appendChild(idCell);

  row.appendChild(sizeCell);

  row.appendChild(solutionCell);

  table.appendChild(row);

 });

 document.body.appendChild(table);

}
printTable(demoPuzzles);
```

Here I think it may have outdone itself. I was expecting to see a bunch of hard-coded strings with HTML characters. I didn't expect it to use DOM manipulation, but of course, that might be the better solution in many cases.

Would Copilot do as well? Actually, it did what I expected originally.

```
// Function to output the puzzles array as an HTML table
printPuzzlesAsHtml() {
  // Get the longest puzzle id, so we can pad the id column to align the puzzle data.
    const longestId = this.demoPuzzles.reduce((longest, puzzle) => Math.max(longest, puzzle.id.toString().length), 0);
  // Print the header row.
  console.log('<table>');
  console.log('<tr><th>id</th><th>size</th><th>solution</th></tr>');
  // Print the puzzle rows.
  this.demoPuzzles.forEach(puzzle => {
    console.log(`<tr><td>${puzzle.id}</td><td>${puzzle.size}</td><td>${puzzle.solution.join(' ')}</
```

```
td></tr>`);
 });
 console.log('</table>');
}
```

That doesn't mean it is incapable of using the DOM API. All I had to do was change my prompt a bit.

```
// Function that uses the DOM API to output the puzzles array as an HTML table
private outputPuzzles(puzzles: Puzzle[]): void {
  const table = document.createElement('table');
  const header = document.createElement('tr');
  header.innerHTML = '<th>ID</th><th>Size</th><th>Solution</th>';
  table.appendChild(header);
  puzzles.forEach(puzzle => {
    const row = document.createElement('tr');
    row.innerHTML = `<td>${puzzle.id}</td><td>${puzzle.size}</td><td>${puzzle.solution}</td>`;
    table.appendChild(row);
  });
  document.body.appendChild(table);
}
```

I'm not sure that's any better. It ended up building me a hybrid of DOM calls and HTML string literals. That's the thing about these AIs; you often have to try the same thing more than once to get the code you're looking for.

Conclusion

This chapter focused primarily on array and string manipulation, which is what most of my day-to-day work entails. You may have different algorithms you work with regularly. Rest assured that either of these tools will save you a lot of typing. The important thing to keep in mind is that the prompt is just as important as the language you ask them to use.

Also, as you've seen, sometimes you have to try multiple prompts to get the right code. Finally, make sure you validate the correctness of the code. Either tool can create code that looks great but doesn't account for edge cases.

Remember that at the end of the day, you're the programmer, not the AI.

LEARNING RXJS

Image by Gerd Altmann from Pixabay

Working with Copilot and ChatGPT on common algorithms got me thinking that they could be very useful tools for learning Reactive Extensions for JavaScript (RxJS), or at least to help me remember some of its non-obvious syntax.

A lot of people don't like to use RxJS, thinking it's too complicated. They tend to avoid it, which I believe is a shame. Yes, RxJS can have a steep learning curve, but learning to think "reactively" and using RxJS effectively has been worth the effort. I wondered how useful Copilot could be in helping others to learn RxJS.

For this chapter, I'm going to continue using that array of puzzles from before. In case you need a refresher, it looks like this:

```
// Partial array of "puzzles" for this example
private demoPuzzles: Puzzle[] = [
  { id:88, size: 4, solution: ['abetbabeebontent'] },
  { id:89, size: 4, solution: ['icedcaveevendent'] },
  { id:90, size: 8, solution: ['abetracemirestun', 'armsbaitecruteen'] },
  { id:91, size: 8, solution: ['cageheaturicmyth', 'chumaerygaitetch'] }
];
```

from and of

Sticking with the above array of puzzles, let's imagine that the puzzles are part of a game, and that they exist as a stream of Observables. Further, assume that the game gets them from some outside source. For now, we won't worry about where they are coming from. Every time a new puzzle is presented, the game will do "something" with it.

So, I asked Copilot to do just that. This is my comment and the code it wrote for me:

```
// Create a new observable from the demo Puzzle array
const puzzles$ = from(this.demoPuzzles);
```

Perfect! The RxJS `from` function creates a new Observable from an array, emitting a new value for each element of the array. That is exactly what I wanted. Notice also that it uses the common naming convention of appending a `$` to the identifier, indicating that it is an Observable.

There is another RxJS operator, `of`, that can also create an Observable from an array. Though it would have been valid to use that, `of` creates a single Observable from that emits once, containing the entire array. That is not what I wanted, and somehow Copilot knew (or guessed) that.

filter

Now that we have an Observable let's do something with it. Let's start with a couple of the simpler and more common RxJS operators: `map` and `filter`.

The RxJS `filter` operator is used to do what its name implies: filter an existing stream to include only those items that match some provided criteria.

What if the game player only wants to see puzzles of size 4? Can we get Copilot to do that for us? Here is the comment I typed and the code Copilot generated in response to that comment:

```
// Filter puzzles to only those of size 4
const size4$ = puzzles$.pipe(filter(puzzle => puzzle.size === 4));
```

What did it give us? It created a new Observable called `size4$`, using the consistent naming convention from before.

It also correctly understands that to use the `filter` operator, we first have to use the RxJS `pipe` function. Any time you are working with an RxJS Observable, and you want to act on it before subscribing to the value stream, you need to pass a list of operators into the `pipe` function.

Next, to select the puzzles of size 4, it correctly deduced that I would need the `filter` operator, which takes a callback function defining how each item in the stream should be matched. If it looks familiar, it's because it works exactly like `Array.filter`.

You might be thinking that I cheated a bit by using the word "Filter" in my comment. What would happen if I used a different phrase? Well, I decided to find out. I deleted the above code and its comment and typed something completely new. I wanted to avoid hinting words like "select" or "filter." This is what it gave me.

```
// Give me only the puzzles of size four
const size4$ = puzzles$.pipe(filter(puzzle => puzzle.size === 4));
```

It still correctly decided that I need to add the `filter` operator to a `pipe` and it converted "four" to 4. Pretty impressive.

map

Let's see what happens if we want only a part of each of the above puzzles. Maybe we are only going to display the first solution of the puzzle as it is emitted.

Any time you want to coerce one object into another, you would first reach for the `map` operator, which works very similarly to the JavaScript Array function of the same name.

As with the prior examples, here are my comment and the generated code:

```
// Display only the first solution of each puzzle
const firstSolution$ = size4$.pipe(map(puzzle => puzzle.solution[0]));
```

Do you see what it did there? It correctly assumed that I would be using the output from the prior command, so it gave me the `size4$` value from before. As I have previously pointed out, this shows that Copilot is aware of the context of your source code.

I think the only disagreement I have is the name `firstSolution$`, but right now I can't think of a better one.

At this point, I have an Observable that is filtered and mapped to only give me the first solution of size-4 puzzles as they are emitted.

Could it combine them for me?

What if I structured my comment to try to get Copilot to write the entire pipeline for me? Let's see how that would look.

```
// Give me the first solution of each size-4 puzzles
puzzles$.pipe(
  filter(puzzle => puzzle.size === 4),
  map(puzzle => puzzle.solution[0]),
  first()
).subscribe(solution => console.log(solution));
```

Honestly, this is close, but it is not what I wanted. I think the word `of` in the comment might have thrown it off. Plus, it insisted on adding the `subscribe`, which I didn't want it to do. When building RxJS solutions, I try not to subscribe because that requires me to remember when I must unsubscribe. I'll touch on that later.

I decided to give it a few more hints to see whether I could help it along. In this case, I typed the comment and `const` on the next line to hint to Copilot I want a constant instead of a subscription.

```
// Give me the first solution for each size-4 puzzles
const
```

```
firstSolution$ = puzzles$.pipe(
  filter(puzzle => puzzle.size === 4),
  map(puzzle => puzzle.solution[0]),
  first()
);
```

Better, but it added `first()`, which I definitely do not want. It's being thrown off by the word "first" in the comment.

Why didn't I want to use `first()`? This operator gives me only the first value from the Observable stream, which is not what I wanted. Instead, I wanted the first puzzle from each value from the stream. A subtle but important difference.

Let's see if I can make a final tweak to get closer.

```
// Give me the first solution inside each puzzle of size four
const firstSolution$ = puzzles$.pipe(
  filter(puzzle => puzzle.size === 4),
  map(puzzle => puzzle.solution[0])
);
```

That's exactly what I wanted it to do. The takeaway for me is that you need to be very specific about your intentions. Don't be afraid to reject its first attempt. You can always try again.

take

The `take` operator is used to select (or take) only a certain number of emissions from the observable and then automatically disconnect. Copilot knew exactly how to structure that for me.

```
// Take only the first two size 8 puzzles
const firstTwoSize8Puzzles$ = this.demoPuzzles$.pipe(
  filter(puzzle => puzzle.size === 8),
  take(2)
);
```

Thinking I might throw it a curveball, so to speak, I asked it to log only those puzzles from the last example. It got it right, building on the code it had just created.

```
// Log the first two size 8 puzzles to the console
firstTwoSize8Puzzles$.subscribe(puzzle => console.log(puzzle));
```

tap

Sometimes you want to see the values in an Observable stream without affecting the stream or any downstream operators. The `tap` operator is built for that exact scenario. Could I get Copilot to rewrite my logging statement above to use tap?

```
// Take the first two size 8 puzzles, but log all puzzles to the console
const demoPuzzles2$ = demoPuzzles$.pipe(
  tap(puzzles => console.log(puzzles)),
  filter(puzzles => puzzles.size === 8),
  take(2)
);
```

That looks just about right, though I'm not thrilled with its naming. In fact, Copilot appears to have remembered that I prefer not to subscribe to my observables, so I'll overlook the odd name.

subscribe

Despite my resistance to using `subscribe` prematurely, could I get Copilot to subscribe to the Observable? Undoubtedly, with the right prompt. As it turns out, as soon as pressed the enter key, Copilot immediately offered the following code with no further action on my part.

```
demoPuzzles2$.subscribe(puzzles => console.log(puzzles));
```

That's exactly what I wanted it to do. I guess it read my mind.

What about ChatGPT for RxJS?

ChatGPT was less of a help for this, but not for the reasons you might expect. At first, I thought it would be better, especially since it tends to explain the code it produces. What bothered me about ChatGPT for RxJS, though, is that it seemed to take me too literally.

For example, when I asked it about using `take` to get me the first two elements, it actually wrote out everything as a complete function. Copilot tends to give you the code you need when you need it.

Where ChatGPT excels is in explaining the code that Copilot writes. Let's see how that would work before moving on. I asked ChatGPT what this code does. It gave me the following analysis, which I'm sure you'll agree is impressive.

What does the following code block do?

```
const firstSolution$ = puzzles$.pipe(
 filter(puzzle => puzzle.size === 4),
 map(puzzle => puzzle.solution[0])
);
```

Sure, the code you provided does the following:

Creates an observable **puzzles$** that emits each element of a larger array of **Puzzle** objects, similar to the **demoPuzzles** array we saw earlier.

Uses the **pipe** method to create a chain of operators that will be applied to each emission of the **puzzles$** observable.

The first operator in the chain is **filter**, which filters out any puzzles that do not have a **size** property of 4. This means that only puzzles with a **size** of 4 will be allowed to continue down the chain.

The second operator in the chain is **map**, which maps each remaining puzzle to its first solution. Since the **solution** property of each **Puzzle** object is an array of strings, we use the array indexing operator **[0]** to select the first element of the array as the solution.

The resulting observable **firstSolution$** emits the first solution of each puzzle that has a **size** of 4.

To summarize, the code filters a stream of **Puzzle** objects by **size** and then maps the remaining puzzles to their first solution, resulting in a stream of strings that represent the first solution of each puzzle that has a **size** of 4.

What's the Takeaway?

Admittedly, there is a lot more to RxJS than the few operators I used here. RxJS is huge, with more than 100 operators, though most developers use fewer than a dozen of them regularly. The goal of this chapter wasn't to perform an exhaustive test of RxJS.

My purpose was to see whether Copilot can help a novice developer get up to speed with RxJS, knowing only a little about what it can do. I will use more RxJS later, where the context is a little more appropriate.

Can Copilot help someone learn RxJS or how to use it better? I'm skeptical, if only because it didn't always give me the code I wanted. An RxJS novice just starting out may not have enough experience to know what to accept and when to try again.

Copilot might be a better option for experienced JavaScript developers who understand the basics of RxJS. They can use it with the reasonable expectation that it will pick the correct operators to match their needs.

Ultimately, while I find Copilot to be a useful and [mostly] benign tool, it does have to be coerced to do the right thing often.

I'm not convinced it's a tool for the RxJS beginner, who may be misled by incorrect code.

ChatGPT, on the other hand, is excellent in helping a novice understand code. Simply paste it into the text box and ask for an explanation. That's powerful and should not be overlooked.

ANGULAR'S HTTPCLIENT

Image by Gerd Altmann from Pixabay

Now let's consider Angular's `HttpClient`, which makes heavy use of RxJS. In fact, the `HttpClient` is often the first place the new Angular developer is introduced to RxJS. That can be a make or break experience.

So, I wanted to see how well it does with some of the common coding patterns we see when using Angular's `HttpClient`.

Even if you aren't an Angular developer, the process is worth understanding.

A Typical Angular Service

For this example, I decided to start with a blank web page and see exactly how little code I could write. Remembering that Copilot needs to know what kind of file it's working on, I immediately told VS Code it was a TypeScript file by clicking on the file type at the bottom right-corner of the window and selecting TypeScript from the options offered.

Next, I entered the following comment at the top of the file:

```
// Provide service in root
```

Copilot immediately gave me three lines:

```
@Injectable({
  providedIn: 'root'
})
```

It stopped there; I presume waiting for me to give it more to go on. I decided not to, and simply pressed the Tab key, to which it responded with this:

```
export class ApiService {
  // API url
  private apiUrl = 'https://api.github.com/users';
  constructor(private http: HttpClient) {}
  // Get user
  getUser(username: string): Observable<User> {
    return this.http.get<User>(`${this.apiUrl}/${username}`);
  }
  // Get repos
  getRepos(username: string): Observable<Repo[]> {
    return this.http.get<Repo[]>
      (`${this.apiUrl}/${username}/repos`);
  }
}
```

That's all pretty cool, but not really what I wanted. I can't complain too much, though, because I didn't give it anything else to go on. I decided to keep the class but remove (for now) the two functions. This left the entire file looking like this:

```
// Provide service in root
@Injectable({
  providedIn: 'root'
}) export class ApiService {
```

```
// API url
private apiUrl = 'https://api.github.com/users';
constructor(private http: HttpClient) {}
}
```

If you're following along, you will notice that Copilot does not automatically import any of those Angular identifiers. The good news is that VS Code will do that for me. Or maybe I could convince Copilot to do it. What if I typed `import` at the top of the file?

When I did that, it didn't do anything. Maybe another hint would help. I added a comment at the top of the file and the word import. Copilot suggested the rest automatically.

```
// Angular service
import { Injectable } from '@angular/core';
import { HttpClient } from '@angular/common/http';
```

Now that the imports were taken care of, I could get on with the rest of the experiment.

A Simple HTTP GET

Whenever I'm building a demo app, I always struggle with where to find decent remote data APIs to showcase. I seldom have the time or inclination to build my own, so I like to look for something interesting, amusing, or both.

If I simply ask Copilot to find me something, what will it provide me? I removed the `apiUrl` variable and its comment. Then added a new comment at the top of the class.

```
// Get some sample data from a remote web server
getSampleData() {
  return this.http.get('https://jsonplaceholder.typicode.com/todos/1');
}
```

That isn't what I expected, but it works. So, I decided to try again with a different prompt.

```
// Get all posts from the API
getAllPosts() {
  return this.http.get('https://jsonplaceholder.typicode.com/posts');
}
```

That's pretty cool and as it turns out, that API is fully functional.

Let's Add Some RxJS

The call to `http.get` returns an Observable, but right now we aren't doing anything with it. What happens if we get an error? I decided to add a hint inside `getAllPosts` to support error handling.

I changed the `return` to a `const posts$` and got this.

```
const posts$ =
this.http.get('https://jsonplaceholder.typicode.com/posts');
// Log any errors from the API call
posts$.subscribe(
  posts => console.log(posts),
  err => console.log(err)
);
```

Ok, that's not what I wanted at all. I was hoping it would suggest using `.pipe` and `.catchError`. I decided to give it a hint by creating a `logError` function, again with Copilot's help.

```
// Log any errors to the console
private handleError(error: any): Promise<any> {
  console.error('An error occurred', error);
  return Promise.reject(error.message || error);
}
```

That felt as though it's gotten worse at guessing my intentions. So, I tried again with a different hint.

```
// Log any errors in the observable to the console
```

```
logError(err) {
  console.error('There was an error: ' + err);
}
```

Better. Well, at least that's what I was going to write. Next, I was curious about Copilot seeing that function in my file and automatically calling it.

```
// Detect and handle errors in the observable stream before returning to the caller.
posts$.subscribe(
  data => console.log(data),
  err => console.error(err),
  () => console.log('done loading posts') // This is called when the observable completes.
);
return posts$;
```

If you were a novice with Angular, its `HttpClient`, or RxJS, you might think this is reasonable code. It's not, at least not in this context. The code block returns an RxJS `Subscription` object, which doesn't work the way the function is written. Most clients would the function to return an `Observable`, that it could subscribe to when convenient.

Before giving up entirely, I decided to try one more thing.

Instead of a comment, I started the next line with `posts$.pipe` and let Copilot suggest the rest. This is what it gave me.

```
posts$.pipe(
  catchError(this.logError));
```

That's what I was looking for!

However, the astute amongst you might have noticed that my `logError` function is no longer valid. I had to change it to return an Observable, but Copilot didn't really help me with that task. I had to do it myself. It now looks like this.

```
// Log any errors in the observable to the console
logError(err): Observable<any> {
  console.error('There was an error: ' + err);
  return of();
```

```
}
```

Using the Observable in the Angular Template

What use is an Observable if we can't get its values? The final example for this chapter is getting the posts from that API call onto a web page. I have to admit, this was pretty interesting.

I started in a blank file and provided the first line below as a comment. It suggested everything else, with only a few hints, which I will explain after the code block.

```
// Angular "Posts" component
import { Component, OnInit } from '@angular/core';
@Component({
  selector: 'app-posts',
  template: `
    <h1>Posts</h1>
    <ul>
      <li *ngFor="let post of posts">
        {{ post.title }}
      </li>
    </ul>
  `,
  styles: []
})
export class PostsComponent implements OnInit {
  posts: any;
  constructor(private apiService: ApiService) { }
  ngOnInit() {
    this.apiService.getAllPosts().subscribe((data) => {
      this.posts = data;
    });
  }
}
```

At first, it wanted a separate file for my template and styles. That's perfectly valid, but overkill for my example. I deleted those lines and manually typed `template` and `styles`. It then added what you see above.

It correctly found and referenced the `ApiService` from the other file, though I did have to fix its import. I consider that a minor nuisance because VS Code will handle that for me.

What about async pipes?

I mentioned before that I prefer not to subscribe to Observables if I don't have to. Angular provides the `async` pipe, which automatically subscribes and unsubscribes as needed. Could I get Copilot to handle that for me?

Following the common practice of naming `Observable` variables with a suffixed dollar sign, I changed the variable name from `posts` to `posts$` and deleted the body of `ngOnInit`.

As soon as I added a blank line inside that function, Copilot suggested exactly what I wanted:

```
ngOnInit() {
  this.posts$ = this.apiService.getAllPosts();
}
```

The only thing left was to see if it would fix the template. So, I went back to the `<li *ngFor` and erased the entire block. Copilot insisted on putting it back the way it was, which wouldn't work at all. There isn't even a variable called `posts`, so it was giving me a literal error.

Not wanting to give up just yet, I added an HTML comment just inside the `<ul>` tag, hoping that would help. That did the trick!

```
<ul>
  <!-- Loop through the posts$ observable and display each post -->
  <li *ngFor="let post of posts$ | async">
    {{ post.title }}
  </li>
</ul>
```

All in all, I was impressed with how well it did once I prompted it with the right hints.

What about ChatGPT?

You may be wondering to yourself, where was ChatGPT throughout all this? Well, because I was staying mostly inside the code editor, I thought that Copilot made more sense for these examples. However, as a test of ChatGPT's capabilities, I asked it to generate everything for me, using my hints to Copilot as my prompt.

Here is the prompt and its complete output.

Build me a complete angular service that fetches some sample data (perhaps blog posts) from a remote web service. Be sure to log any errors encountered. Then create a web page implemented as an angular component, which displays the blog post titles from the service in an unordered list. Prefer to use the angular async pipe in the template rather than subscribing to the observable.

Sure, I'd be happy to help you with that! Here is an example implementation of an Angular service and component that fetches blog posts from a remote web service:

```typescript
import { Injectable } from '@angular/core';
import { HttpClient } from '@angular/common/http';
import { Observable, throwError } from 'rxjs';
import { catchError } from 'rxjs/operators';

@Injectable({
  providedIn: 'root'
})
export class BlogPostService {
  private apiUrl = 'https://jsonplaceholder.typicode.com/posts';
  constructor(private http: HttpClient) { }
  getBlogPosts(): Observable<any[]> {
    return this.http.get<any[]>(this.apiUrl).pipe(
      catchError(error => {
        console.error('Error fetching blog posts:', error);
        return throwError(error);
      })
```

```
    );
  }
}
```

This service uses the **HttpClient** module from Angular to make an HTTP GET request to the specified API URL. If an error occurs during the request, the service logs the error to the console and throws an error using the **throwError** method from the **rxjs** library.

```
import { Component, OnInit } from '@angular/core';
import { Observable } from 'rxjs';
import { BlogPostService } from '../blog-post.service';
@Component({
 selector: 'app-blog-post-list',
 template: `
  <h2>Blog Posts</h2>
  <ul>
   <li *ngFor="let post of posts$ | async">{{ post.title }}</li>
  </ul>
  `
})
export class BlogPostListComponent implements OnInit {
 posts$: Observable<any[]>;
 constructor(private blogPostService: BlogPostService) { }
 ngOnInit(): void {
  this.posts$ = this.blogPostService.getBlogPosts();
 }
}
```

This component uses the **async** pipe in the template to subscribe to the **posts$** observable returned by the **BlogPostService**. The **ngOnInit** method of the component sets the **posts$** observable to the result of calling **getBlogPosts** on the service.

> Finally, you'll need to add the **HttpClientModule** to your app module's imports array to make the **HttpClient** available to the service:

```
import { NgModule } from '@angular/core';
import { BrowserModule } from '@angular/platform-browser';
import { HttpClientModule } from '@angular/common/http';
import { AppComponent } from './app.component';
import { BlogPostListComponent } from './blog-post-list/blog-post-list.component';
@NgModule({
  declarations: [
    AppComponent,
    BlogPostListComponent
  ],
  imports: [
    BrowserModule,
    HttpClientModule
  ],
  providers: [],
  bootstrap: [AppComponent]
})
export class AppModule { }
```

> That's it! With this code, you should be able to display a list of blog post titles retrieved from a remote web service in an Angular component using the **async** pipe.

Wow! ChatGPT built almost exactly the same code, complete with explanations. In fact, what it produced is more complete than what I got from Copilot.

My only complaint about what it wrote is that its information is slightly outdated. Angular 14.2 introduced a developer preview of "standalone components," which don't need to be contained inside an `NgModule`. You can even write entire applications without a single `NgModule`. Angular 15 officially made them part of the framework.

This is a minor thing, but it serves to illustrate an important point. ChatGPT's knowledge doesn't know much about the past 2 years. I asked ChatGPT to rewrite the above application with standalone components from Angular 15. This was its reply.

> I'm sorry, but Angular 15 is not a version that exists - the latest version of Angular as of my knowledge cutoff date of September 2021 is Angular 12. However, I can provide an example of how to rewrite the application using Angular's componentless routes with the **ng-container** element, introduced in Angular 4.

It then proceeded to give me almost the same application as before but adding in some default routing. Angular 12 is 3 versions old as I write this, soon to be 4 versions old. I don't even think it's supported anymore.

Let this be a friendly reminder and warning. ChatGPT is amazing at what it does, if you're looking for information that tends to be long-lived. That's why it does so well with regular expressions, scripting, and common algorithms. By its own admission, its knowledge can be woefully outdated, especially in this industry, which moves as fast as it does.

REGULAR EXPRESSIONS

Image by Author and OpenAI

Input validation is a critical component of ensuring data integrity and preventing security vulnerabilities. However, crafting effective regular expressions (regexes) can be a time-consuming and challenging task. That's where Copilot and ChatGPT come in. In this chapter, I set out to explore how well they could generate regexes for input validation using nothing more than a simple prompt in the form of a comment. Read on to discover my findings and the surprising effectiveness of this AI-powered tool.

Regex 101 Site

I decided to use an existing regex website to help me test what Copilot provided: regex101: build, test, and debug regex. (https://regex101.com)

This site lets me choose what type of regular expression to test and has some really cool error detection and debugging features.

Email Address

The first thing that came to mind is evaluating a string to see if it is a valid email address.

I asked Copilot to make an email pattern for me inside a TypeScript file. This is what it gave me.

```
// Email regex
emailRegex = /^((([^<>()\[\]\\.,;:\s@"]+(\.[^<>()\[\]\\.,;:\s@"]+)*)|(".+"))@((\[[0-9]{1,3}\.[0-9]{1,3}\.[0-9]{1,3}\.[0-9]{1,3}\])|(([a-zA-Z\-0-9]+\.)+[a-zA-Z]{2,}))$/;
```

It looks clever, but does it work? Dropping that into regex101.com, I was able to test some emails fairly quickly. Here are some other email addresses I tried:

Matched

mike@company.com
mike@company.co.uk
x@y.com
mike@x.cc

Not Matched

mike@localhost
mike@10.0.0.1
mike@x.
Bill

The first two of those are valid, but Copilot's regex failed to match them. Would ChatGPT do any better?

```
Give me a regular expression to validate an email address

^[a-zA-Z0-9._%+-]+@[a-zA-Z0-9.-]+\.[a-zA-Z]{2,}$
```

This one looks nothing like what Copilot gave me. Does it do any better with my test email addresses? As it turns out, it matched exactly the same. ChatGPT provided a lengthy explanation of the regex it gave me, which I won't reproduce here. Suffice it to say that it was complete.

So, they aren't bad, but I'm wondering how they stack up to the professionals.

According to a an article I found on the most comprehensive email regex, this is "the best" email pattern:

```
([-!#-'*+/-9=?A-Z^-~]+(\.[-!#-'*+/-9=?A-Z^-~]+)*|"([]!#-[^-~ \t]|(\\[\t -~]))+")@([0-9A-Za-z]([0-9A-Za-z-]{0,61}[0-9A-Za-z])?(\.[0-9A-Za-z]([0-9A-Za-z-]{0,61}[0-9A-Za-z])?)*|\[(((25[0-5]|2[0-4][0-9]|1[0-9]{2}|[1-9]?[0-9])(\.(25[0-5]|2[0-4][0-9]|1[0-9]{2}|[1-9]?[0-9])){3}|IPv6:((((0|[1-9A-Fa-f][0-9A-Fa-f]{0,3}):){6}|::((0|[1-9A-Fa-f][0-9A-Fa-f]{0,3}):){5}|[0-9A-Fa-f]{0,4}::((0|[1-9A-Fa-f][0-9A-Fa-f]{0,3}):){4}|((0|[1-9A-Fa-f][0-9A-Fa-f]{0,3}):)?(0|[1-9A-Fa-f][0-9A-Fa-f]{0,3}))?::((0|[1-9A-Fa-f][0-9A-Fa-f]{0,3}):){3}|(((0|[1-9A-Fa-f][0-9A-Fa-f]{0,3}):){0,2}(0|[1-9A-Fa-f][0-9A-Fa-f]{0,3}))?::((0|[1-9A-Fa-f][0-9A-Fa-f]{0,3}):){2}|(((0|[1-9A-Fa-f][0-9A-Fa-f]{0,3}):){0,3}(0|[1-9A-Fa-f][0-9A-Fa-f]{0,3}))?::(0|[1-9A-Fa-f][0-9A-Fa-f]{0,3}):|(((0|[1-9A-Fa-f][0-9A-Fa-f]{0,3}):){0,4}(0|[1-9A-Fa-f][0-9A-Fa-f]{0,3}))?::)(0|[1-9A-Fa-f][0-9A-Fa-f]{0,3}):(0|[1-9A-Fa-f][0-9A-Fa-f]{0,3})|(25[0-5]|2[0-4][0-9]|1[0-9]{2}|[1-9]?[0-9])(\.(25[0-5]|2[0-4][0-9]|1[0-9]{2}|[1-9]?[0-9])){3})|(((0|[1-9A-Fa-f][0-9A-Fa-f]{0,3}):){0,5}(0|[1-9A-Fa-f][0-9A-Fa-f]{0,3}))?::(0|[1-9A-Fa-f][0-9A-Fa-f]{0,3})|(((0|[1-9A-Fa-f][0-9A-Fa-f]{0,3}):){0,6}(0|[1-9A-Fa-f][0-9A-Fa-f]{0,3}))?::)|(?!IPv6:)[0-9A-Za-z-]*[0-9A-Za-z]:[!-Z^-~]+)])
```

That's a 1240-character regex! It looks nothing like the one the AIs gave me.

This one did much better, including matching two valid email addresses from the above list that the first regex did not.

mike@localhost
mike@10.0.0.1

Honestly, I think that both regexes from the AI are fine, but they did miss those two valid email addresses.

Phone numbers

Moving on, how well will they do validating a phone number? I gave Copilot a comment hint to see what it came up with and it gave me this at first.

```
// Phone number pattern with optional country code
phoneRegex = /^(\+?1)?[2-9]\d{2}[2-9](?!11)\d{6}$/;
```

This one sort of works, but it doesn't allow any punctuation or spacing in the number. It does allow an optional +1, but that only works for US phone numbers.

Matched

2025551212
8002822882
+12025551212

+14079393463

Not matched

603–555–1212
603 555 1212
(603) 555 1212

Not to be completely daunted yet, I thought I'd give it one more try. I gave it a different comment:

```
// international phone number
phoneRegex = /^\+?([0-9]{2})\)?[-. ]?([0-9]{3})[-. ]?([0-9]{3})[-. ]?([0-9]{4})$/;
```

This one was a lot more flexible, but it still failed to match what I would consider some common phone number formats:

Matched

+01 202 555 1212
+014079393463

// UK Number
+44 889 234 1239
+44.889.234.1239
+44 889–234–1239

Not Matched

(202) 555–1212
800–282–2882

So far, I am not impressed with what Copilot gave me. ChatGPT gave me this one:

```
Give me a regex that can validate any phone number, us or international, liberally accepting common punctuation.

^[\+]?[\d]{0,3}[\s.-]?[\(]?[\d]{1,3}[\)]?[\s.-]?[\d]{3,4}[\s.-]?[\d]{3,4}$
```

It actually did worse, matching only the first two UK numbers, and failing the same ones Copilot's pattern did. Maybe matching a phone number is simply too difficult with a regex.

Valid URL

Related to, though not specifically about validation, I wanted to see whether Copilot would give me a pattern to recognize valid all URLs inside a string. That could be useful for crawling websites. As with the rest of the examples, I started with a comment. It gave me two options:

```
// Regex to find URLs inside a string
urlRegex = /((https?:\/\/)|(www\.))[^\s]+/g;
urlRegex = /((https?:\/\/)?[\w-]+(\.[\w-]+)+\.?(:\d+)?(\/\S*)?)/g;
```

What I find really cool about these suggestions is that Copilot gave me the `g` modifier (match globally) on both regexes, presumably because I asked for `URLs` (plural) in my comment, and not simply the singular `URL`.

The first one, though it looks OK at first glance, is simply wrong. My test string was the source code of a web page with lots of links. The first regex gave me 137 matches, but upon further inspection, it included punctuation that was part of the surrounding text and NOT part of the URL.

So, I decided to try the second, longer suggestion. That one was actually worse, matching a bunch of text that clearly are not URLs. What bothers me about both of these regexes is that they match the closing quote in an HTML attribute.

```
<img src="https://pictures.com/images/12345.jpg">
```

According to both regexes, the URL portion of that img tag is `https://pictures.com/images/12345.jpg"`

It made me think that perhaps my comment hint was wrong. Instead of searching for URLs in a "string," maybe I should be more specific. I decided to give it one more shot.

```
// Regex to find all URLs from img and a tags
urlRegex = /<img[^>]*src="([^"]*)"[^>]*>|<a[^>]*href="([^"]*)"[^>]*>/g;
```

Interestingly enough, I believe this one came closest. Notice that my comment was a lot more specific about what I was looking for. What's more, I had to look a little more closely at the matches. The actual URLs are inside of Group 2 of each match.

ChatGPT took me literally, as it has been doing throughout all my research and experimentation.

> Give me a regex to find all URLs from img and a tags in the text of an HTML page.
>
> (?<=<img.*?src="|<a.*?href=")[^"]*

It did not give me a regex looking to match URLs. Instead, it is a regex that extracts the entire string inside the quotes following an `img` or `href` attribute. That is, in fact, exactly what I asked for.

Not giving up just yet, I offered a more explicit prompt to ChatGPT to tweak its understanding.

> Give me a regex matching URLs found in an arbitrary document of text, which may or may not be HTML.
>
> \b(?:(?:https?|ftp):\/\/|www\.)[^\s]+\b

Its explanation was comprehensive, so I tested it and discovered that it was by far the best regular expression. This would be a better regex to use if you were validating that a given string is, in fact, a URL.

Password complexity

Just about every web site that lets users register has some rule about password complexity. Can Copilot generate a regex to validate such passwords?

> // Passwords much contain at least one number, one lowercase and one uppercase letter, one symbol, and be 8 characters or longer.
>
> private passwordRegex = /^(?=.*[a-z])(?=.*[A-Z])(?=.*\d)(?=.*[^\da-zA-Z]).{8,}$/;

That's quite the regex, but is it correct? Back over at regex101.com, I put it to the test.

Valid Passwords

P@55word
This1s@GoodPassword
MikeWasHerein1999!

Invalid Passwords

password
MikeWasHere!
This is a bad password
12345

My hastily-considered opinion is that this is a good regex for its purpose.

ChatGPT gave me a functionally similar, but slightly different pattern.

> *Give me a regex to validate password complexity with the following rules: Passwords much contain at least one number, one lowercase and one uppercase letter, one symbol, and be 8 characters or longer.*
>
> ^(?=.*\d)(?=.*[a-z])(?=.*[A-Z])(?=.*\W)[\S]{8,}$

It matched the same password list as Copilot's regular expression, so I consider them both valid.

Valid U.S. currency

Another common scenario is determining whether or not input is valid US currency.

```
// Validate that the input is a US currency
private currencyRegex = /^\$?(([1-9]\d{0,2}(,\d{3})*)|0)?(\.\d{2})?$/;
```

This one looks good at first glance. I tried a short list of strings that I imagine people might enter into a web page as currency. Let's see how that regex did.

Valid Currency

$1
.22
$.25
0.79
1.49
$0.00
$0.43
$1,230,847,369.99

Invalid Currency

Mike
1.575
1.57$
2.25%
1 dollar

Looks pretty good to me. I'd call that a pass.

ChatGPT gave me a similar regex.

> *Give me a regex that will validate that the input is a US currency*
>
> `^\$[1-9]\d{0,2}(,\d{3})*(\.\d{2})?$`

Unfortunately, it failed all the test values except the first and last valid values. I asked it to try again, allowing for an optional dollar sign. The regex it gave me validated only one additional test value (1.49) but still failed on the rest.

Giving it one more chance, I decided to take a different approach. Here is my entire conversation and its reply.

> *Given a potential list of different ways to write US currency, write a regular expression that will match all of these: $1 .22 $.25 0.79 1.49 $0.00 $0.43 $1,230,847,369.99*
>
> Here's a regular expression that can match all of the given examples of US currency values:
>
> `^(?:\$\s?)?(?:\d{1,3}(?:,\d{3})*|\d+)(?:\.\d{2})?$`
>
> Let's break down this regular expression:
>
> **^** - Start of the line
>
> **(?:\$\s?)?** - Optionally match a dollar sign followed by an optional whitespace character
>
> **(?:\d{1,3}(?:,\d{3})*|\d+)** - Match either a sequence of 1-3 digits, optionally followed by groups of three digits separated by commas, or a single sequence of one or more digits.
>
> **(?:\.\d{2})?** - Optionally match a period followed by exactly two digits
>
> **$** - End of the line
>
> This regular expression matches the given examples of US currency values, including dollar amounts with or without the dollar sign, decimal points and commas.
>
> Note that this regular expression does not match negative amounts. Also, if you have currency values with unusual formats, such as negative amounts or amounts with more than two decimal places, you may need to modify the regular expression accordingly.

How well do you think it did?

It got all of them except the $.25 value. Not bad, but it shows that ChatGPT isn't infallible. However, I do appreciate the power of giving it examples and letting it do the rest.

U.S. Social Security Number

What about social security numbers? Those are pretty straightforward in the US, so I didn't expect too much of a challenge here.

```
// Validate the the input is a valid SSN
private ssnRegex = /^\d{3}-?\d{2}-?\d{4}$/;
```

Valid SSN

999–99–9999
012–34–5678
978–76–5432

Invalid SSN

978 76 5432
97–876–5432
5432–76–978
xxx-yy-zzzz

As I said, pretty straightforward. ChatGPT went above and beyond in its reply.

```
Write a regex that will validate the the input is a valid SSN.
^(?!000)(?!666)[0-8]\d{2}[- ]?(?!00)\d{2}[- ]?(?!0000)\d{4}$
```

This regex ensures that certain SSNs are specifically disallowed. ChatGPT also provided this warning, which I found both useful and amusing.

> Note that this regular expression only checks the format of the SSN, not whether it is an actual valid SSN that is assigned to a specific person. It's also worth noting that some SSNs assigned before June 25, 2011 may not be valid, as the Social Security Administration implemented a new randomization policy on that date.

I didn't know any of that trivia around social security numbers.

Valid credit card numbers

I expected that this one might pose a little more of a challenge. Validating credit card numbers is a common task for web apps. However, relying solely on regular expressions (regex) to validate credit card numbers can be dangerous. While regex is a powerful tool for pattern matching, it may not catch all potential errors or security risks associated with credit card numbers.

This is because credit card numbers have a complex structure with multiple rules and restrictions, and regex patterns may not always account for all of them. Credit card numbers are not simply a pattern of grouped digits, though they may appear to be at first glance. I don't think a regex can compute the checksum (aka Luhn Algorithm), so I think we may have to settle for "close."

```
// Validate the credit card number
private creditCardRegex = /^((4\d{3})|(5[1-5]\d{2})|(6011))(-?\d{4}){3}$/;
```

That regex might be good for a first-pass client-side validation, but it's far from perfect.

Valid CC#

4321567843215678
6011222233334444
4444333322221111
5432123456789999

Invalid CC#

4321 5678 4321 5678
6011 2222 3333 4444
4444 3333 2222 1111
5432 1234 5678 9999
378282246310005 (Valid Amex)

That last one is a false negative. Apparently, the regex cannot match American Express card numbers.

One last thought I had was whether or not Copilot knows what the Lunh Algorithm is. The JavaScript is available on the developer page I linked above.

I got this response when I typed my comment, which is not what I expected:

```
// Validate the credit card number using the Lunh Algorithm
private creditCardLuhnRegex = /^(?:4[0-9]{12}(?:[0-9]{3})?|5[1-5][0-9]{14}|3[47][0-9]{13}|3(?:0[0-5]|[68][0-9])[0-9]{11}|6(?:011|5[0-9][0-9])[0-9]{12}|(?:2131|1800|35\d{3})\d{11})$/;
```

It doesn't actually appear to implement the algorithm, but it does match the Amex number that the first regex missed.

Before leaving this section, I wondered if a slight change to my comment might make it work.

```
// Function to Validate the credit card number using the Lunh Algorithm
private validateCreditCardNumber(cardNumber: string): boolean {
  let sum = 0;
  let shouldDouble = false;
  for (let i = cardNumber.length - 1; i >= 0; i--) {
    let digit = parseInt(cardNumber.charAt(i), 10);
    if (shouldDouble) {
      if ((digit *= 2) > 9) digit -= 9;
    }
    sum += digit;
    shouldDouble = !shouldDouble;
  }
  return sum % 10 === 0;
} // End of validateCreditCardNumber
```

I didn't run it to test it out, but that is a lot closer to what I was expecting. Feel free to give it a try.

I suspected that ChatGPT would be better for this sort of thing, so I gave it a similar prompt to see what it would come up with.

Implement a function to validate a credit card number using the Lunh Algorithm

Sure, here's a Python function that uses the Luhn Algorithm to validate a credit card number:

```python
def validate_credit_card_number(card_number):
    # Reverse the credit card number and convert each digit to an integer
    digits = [int(x) for x in str(card_number)][::-1]
    # Double the value of every second digit
    doubled_digits = []
    for i, digit in enumerate(digits):
        if i % 2 == 1:
            doubled_digits.append(digit * 2)
        else:
            doubled_digits.append(digit)
```

```python
    # Add the digits of the doubled values and the undoubled digits
    total = 0
    for digit in doubled_digits:
        if digit > 9:
            total += digit - 9
        else:
            total += digit
    # If the total is a multiple of 10, the card number is valid
    return total % 10 == 0
```

Does it work? I don't really know. Honestly, I didn't test it. I don't speak Python, but it did give me a glimpse at some of the languages the ChatGPT (and presumably Copilot) knows. The JavaScript I got from Copilot looks different from the JavaScript code at the website.

If you decide to test either version, let me know if it works.

HTML tags

Can Copilot recognize legal HTML tags?

```
// Recognize all HTML tags in the input text
private htmlTagRegex = /<[^>]*>/g;
```

I won't show the matches here, but this one seems to work. My only complaint is that it sees closing tags, too.

ChatGPT decided that I still wanted Python, based on the last conversation I had with it. This is another reminder that your conversations have context that ChatGPT will remember.

```
Write a regex to recognize all HTMl tags in the input text.
import re
pattern = r'<\/?[a-zA-Z]+\b(?:\s*[a-zA-Z]+=(?:"[^"]*"|\'[^\']*\'))*\s*\/?>'
tags = re.findall(pattern, input_text)
```

> *Go back to giving me raw regexes, not wrapped in python*
>
> `<\/?[a-zA-Z]+\b(?:\s*[a-zA-Z]+=(?:"[^"]*"|\'[^\']*\'))*\s*\/?>`

They appear to be the same regex, with the former wrapped in Python syntax.

Detect Repeated Words

How hard would it be to detect repeated words in a piece of text?

> `// Find repeated words in the input text`
>
> `private repeatedWordRegex = /\b(\w+)\b\s+\b\1\b/g;`

I expected this one to be more complicated than it was, but on reflection, this is the kind of thing regular expressions really good for. ChatGPT gave me almost the exact same pattern, except it appears to account for duplicate words that are separated by punctuation.

> `\b(\w+)\b(?=.*\b\1\b)`
>
> Note that this regular expression will not match repeated words that are separated by non-word characters (e.g., "hello, hello" will not match). If you want to match repeated words regardless of the characters separating them, you can replace the word boundary **\b** with a whitespace character **\s** in the regular expression.

Repeated Words Detected

Mike was was here here
the quick brown fox fox jumps over the lazy dog
Space, the the final frontier

Repeated Words Not Detected

mike was here
mike was here was here
Space, The the final frontier
the quick brown fox jumps over the lazy dog

You may notice that the regex is case-sensitive. Adding an `i` should solve that problem.

Valid JavaScript identifiers

This one made sense after I saw what it wrote, but it wasn't what I expected (honestly, I'm not sure what I expected).

```
// Recognize all valid JavaScript keywords in the input text
private jsKeywordRegex = /\b(break|case|catch|continue|debugger|default|delete|do|else|finally|for|
function|if|in|instanceof|new|return|switch|this|throw|try|typeof|var|void|while|with|class|const|
enum|export|extends|import|super|implements|interface|let|package|private|protected|public|
static|yield|abstract|boolean|byte|char|double|final|float|goto|int|long|native|short|synchronized|
throws|transient|volatile)\b/g;
```

ChatGPT gave me practically the same regex.

```
\b(?:await|break|case|catch|class|const|continue|debugger|default|delete|do|else|enum|export|
extends|false|finally|for|function|if|implements|import|in|instanceof|interface|let|new|null|
package|private|protected|public|return|super|switch|this|throw|true|try|typeof|var|void|while|
with|yield)\b
```

Looking at both patterns more closely, I'm not convinced that either of them is 100% correct, though.

Conclusion

After some early failures, I think it's safe to say that both ChatGPT and Copilot *can help* with regular expressions. However, as you have seen, they are both far from perfect.

As with any code written for you by an AI (or even other developers), you can't simply accept what you're given without question. It's important to understand what the code does.

As I have written previously, I will continue to use them where it makes sense. I will not, however, blindly use everything written for me by an AI.

DATA GENERATION

Image by Thorsten Frenzel from Pixabay

Never Lack Sample Data for Your Apps

Generating sample data is a crucial aspect of application development, as it allows developers to test and refine their software in a controlled environment. In this chapter, we will explore the effectiveness of Copilot and ChatGPT in generating sample data for applications. We will start with simple examples and gradually move towards more complex ideas, sharing both the successes and failures along the way. By the end of this chapter, you will have a better understanding of the capabilities and limitations of these tools and how they can be leveraged to improve your application development process.

As before I will show my simple comment, followed by what the AIs suggested, with commentary where appropriate.

Lorem Ipsum Text

First, let's see what Copilot suggested for a generic request for some "lorem ipsum" text.

```
// Generate a paragraph of lorem ipsum text
const text = require('lorem-ipsum').loremIpsum({count: 1, units: 'paragraphs'});
```

That isn't what I expected at all. I had hoped it would simply build some for me. Honestly, I'd never heard of a lorem-ipsum npm package, so I decided to look for it. I installed the package and ran my code, which output this:

> Aliquip qui est officia tempor elit aliquip. Lorem culpa ea exercitation aliqua aliquip et aute. Eiusmod ad sunt labore proident id reprehenderit ullamco dolore laborum excepteur ad eiusmod laboris. Et duis consectetur culpa nulla velit adipisicing minim velit dolore deserunt commodo id occaecat. Mollit aliquip consectetur aliquip duis eu incididunt ut amet deserunt qui.

Again, not what I expected, but it did the right thing. I can hardly complain when it gives me working code.

ChatGPT did exactly what I expected without any additional prompting. It just worked.

> Lorem ipsum dolor sit amet, consectetur adipiscing elit. Sed auctor, purus non ornare congue, magna magna porta velit, eget malesuada velit velit vel mi. Sed velit velit, suscipit vel dolor eu, malesuada ornare elit. Sed dictum id elit vel dictum. Donec malesuada risus vitae ipsum placerat, eget aliquam velit ullamcorper. Sed in eros vel velit blandit elementum. Sed nec tempor tellus. Sed non eros euismod, feugiat eros ut, gravida dolor. Nam auctor malesuada est, euismod euismod erat tempor id.

List of schools in the USA

For the next experiment, I wanted a list of schools that can be found in the United States. This one took on the same pattern as above, but with a different outcome.

```
// List of schools in the USA
```

```
const schools = require('us-schools').schools;
console.log(schools);
```

Unfortunately, no such npm package exists, at least not that I could find. I was starting to have less faith in this process than when I began.

On the other hand, ChatGPT again came through.

Give me a list of schools in the USA as a JavaScript array

```
const schools = [
  { name: "Harvard University", state: "Massachusetts" },
  { name: "Stanford University", state: "California" },
  { name: "Princeton University", state: "New Jersey" },
  { name: "Yale University", state: "Connecticut" },
  { name: "Columbia University", state: "New York" },
  { name: "Brown University", state: "Rhode Island" },
  { name: "University of Pennsylvania", state: "Pennsylvania" },
  { name: "Cornell University", state: "New York" },
  { name: "Dartmouth College", state: "New Hampshire" }
];
```

Fake Customers with Addresses

Wondering whether I would ever get a success out of Copilot, I moved on with my preplanned list. Could it generate some fake customers for me?

```
// Generate a list of random customer names and addresses
const faker = require('faker');
const customers = [];
for (let i = 0; i < 100; i++) {
  customers.push({
    name: faker.name.findName(),
    address: faker.address.streetAddress(),
    city: faker.address.city(),
```

```
  state: faker.address.state(),
  zip: faker.address.zipCode(),
});
}
```

I've used faker (https://www.npmjs.com/package/@faker-js/faker) in the past, so I had higher hopes for this one. I installed the faker npm package and added a `console.table(customers)` command. This would print the array to my browser console in a grid, with each "customer" on its own row.

That gave me errors, as the `require` line is incorrect. The correct version is

```
const { faker } = require('@faker-js/faker');
```

Once I fixed that, I was informed that `findName` has been deprecated in favor of `fullName`, but the code still runs. I was provided with an output of fake customers.

> *GitHub Copilot was trained on years and years of existing code, so it makes sense that some of that code will be based on older patterns or deprecated libraries. It's inevitable, but the good news is that as we continue to train it, it'll only get better.*

Given what you've already seen, you probably have more faith in ChatGPT in getting this right. If you were to bet on it, you would have lost.

```
Generate a list of random customer names and addresses
const faker = require('faker');
let customers = [];
for(let i = 0; i < 10; i++) {
  let customer = {
    name: faker.name.findName(),
    address: faker.address.streetAddress()
  }
  customers.push(customer);
```

```
}
console.log(customers);
```

ChatGPT made the exact same mistakes as Copilot. This is not entirely unexpected, as the data on which ChatGPT was trained ended sometime in 2021. It isn't aware of any updates to libraries and frameworks made after that. What is less expected is that it wrote code that was almost identical to Copilot.

Not completely undaunted, I made a slight change and asked ChatGPT to try again, without `faker`. I wanted to see whether it could do it on its own. I got more than I expected, but it did what I asked.

```
Generate a list of random customer names and addresses without using the faker library
let customers = []
const firstNames = ['John', 'Emily', 'Jessica', 'Michael', 'David',
        'Jacob', 'Madison', 'Ethan', 'Elizabeth']
const lastNames = ['Smith', 'Johnson', 'Williams', 'Jones', 'Brown',
        'Miller', 'Wilson', 'Moore', 'Taylor']
const streets = ['Main St', 'High St', 'Park Ave', '1st St', '2nd St',
    '4th St', '5th St', '6th St', '7th St']
const cities = ['New York', 'Los Angeles', 'Chicago', 'Houston',
        'Philadelphia', 'San Antonio', 'San Diego', 'Dallas']
const states = ['NY', 'CA', 'TX', 'AZ', 'PA', 'TX', 'CA', 'TX', 'CA']
const zipCodes = ['10001', '90001', '60601', '77001', '85001', '19019',
        '78201', '92201', '75201', '95201']
for(let i = 0; i < 10; i++) {
  let customer = {
    name: firstNames[Math.floor(Math.random() * firstNames.length)] +
       ' ' + lastNames[Math.floor(Math.random() * lastNames.length)],
    address: streets[Math.floor(Math.random() * streets.length)] + ' ' +
            cities[Math.floor(Math.random() * cities.length)] + ' ' +
```

```
            states[Math.floor(Math.random() * states.length)] + ' ' +
        zipCodes[Math.floor(Math.random() * zipCodes.length)]
    }
    customers.push(customer)
}
```

Another interesting thing about this particular code generation: I asked ChatGPT to wrap at 60 characters and to use single quotes instead of double quotes, which it did.

Random Color generation

Have you ever needed some random colors? I admit this one is a bit less impressive, but I was determined to continue. My hypothesis at this point is that Copilot would continue to use `faker`.

```
// Add a random color to each customer

const colors = ['red', 'green', 'blue', 'yellow', 'orange', 'purple'];
for (const customer of customers) {
  customer.color = colors[Math.floor(Math.random() * colors.length)];
}
```

But, of course, I was wrong. This is closer to what I expected it to do before it started using `faker`. I was hoping to get some CSS colors instead of names.

```
// Add a favorite CSS Color to each customer
for (const customer of customers) {
  customer.color = faker.commerce.color();
}
```

What? It went back to using `faker`! This is fine, but `commerce.color()` apparently is deprecated also. Copilot never suggested using the newer functions. It worked, though, which might be all we can expect.

ChatGPT took that comment and rewrote its entire code block, adding the new functionality where appropriate. Here are the relevant lines it added:

```
Add a random color to each customer
```

```
const colors = ['Red', 'Green', 'Blue', 'Orange', 'Yellow', 'Purple', 'Pink', 'Brown', 'Gray', 'Black']
for(let i = 0; i < 10; i++) {
  let customer = {
    ...
    color: colors[Math.floor(Math.random() * colors.length)]
  }
  customers.push(customer)
}
console.log(customers)
```

Would it do as well if I asked it to use CSS colors? It came through perfectly, changing the above colors array to a `colorValues` array.

```
Add a favorite CSS Color to each customer
const colorValues = ['#ff0000', '#00ff00', '#0000ff', '#ffa500',
       '#ffc0cb', '#a52a2a', '#808080', '#000000']
```

Notice that ChatGPT doesn't use semicolons in its generated code. I don't know what to make of that, but if you want it to include them, you can simply ask it to do so.

By the way, ChatGPT is happy to use the faker library to generate colors. I won't include that code here, as it is still insisting on using a version that doesn't work.

As I have said before, this stuff isn't perfect.

Movie titles

What about movie titles? Would they be able to generate real movies or real-sounding fake movies?

```
// Add a favorite movie to each customer
for (const customer of customers) {
  customer.movie = faker.commerce.productName();
}
```

Apparently, faker doesn't know anything about movies, and Copilot was unable (or unwilling) to suggest anything else.

I consider this one a failure, at least for Copilot.

ChatGPT did exactly what I had hoped it would do from the beginning. It gave me an array of movie titles.

```
// Add a favorite movie to each customer
const movies = ['The Godfather', 'The Shawshank Redemption', 'The Dark Knight', 'The Good, the Bad and the Ugly', 'The Lord of the Rings: The Return of the King', 'Pulp Fiction', 'The Matrix', 'Goodfellas', 'One Flew Over the Cuckoo\'s Nest', 'Seven Samurai']
```

Then, it added a random element from that array into each customer (not shown).

Given the movie list, I didn't have high hopes for Copilot to handle the rest of my list. My expectations for ChatGPT were still pretty high, though. I will present the rest of them here without comment unless the results were way out of line with my (by now meager) expectations.

Car Makes and Models

Copilot

```
// What kind of car does each customer drive?
for (const customer of customers) {
  customer.car = faker.vehicle.model();
}
```

ChatGPT

It gave me another array from which it would randomly assign a car.

```
What kind of car does each customer drive?
const cars = ['Ford', 'Chevrolet', 'Toyota', 'Honda', 'Nissan', 'Jeep', 'Dodge', 'Chrysler', 'BMW', 'Mercedes-Benz']
```

Dog breeds

Copilot

```
// What kind of dog does each customer have?
for (const customer of customers) {
```

```
  customer.dog = faker.animal.dog();
}
```

ChatGPT

What kind of dog does each customer have?

```
const dogs = ['Golden Retriever', 'Labrador Retriever', 'German Shepherd', 'Bulldog', 'Poodle', 'Beagle', 'Rottweiler', 'Yorkshire Terrier']
```

Deck of cards

Copilot

```
// Create a random deck of cards
const deck = [];
const suits = ['Hearts', 'Diamonds', 'Spades', 'Clubs'];
const ranks = ['Ace', '2', '3', '4', '5', '6', '7', '8', '9', '10', 'Jack', 'Queen', 'King'];
for (const suit of suits) {
  for (const rank of ranks) {
    deck.push({ suit, rank });
  }
}
```

This wasn't bad and it's accurate. Next, we might want to shuffle the deck.

```
// Shuffle the deck
deck.sort(() => Math.random() - 0.5);
```

Not bad. And it didn't use `faker`.

ChatGPT

ChatGPT did a similar job and added some explanation, which as we have seen, is typical for its output.

```
// Create an array of all possible card values
const cardValues = ['Ace', 'Two', 'Three', 'Four', 'Five', 'Six', 'Seven', 'Eight', 'Nine', 'Ten', 'Jack', 'Queen', 'King'];
```

```
// Create an array of all possible card suits
const cardSuits = ['Hearts', 'Diamonds', 'Spades', 'Clubs'];
// Create an empty array to store the random deck of cards
const randomDeck = [];
// Loop through each card value and suit, creating a new card object and pushing it to the randomDeck array
for (let i = 0; i < cardValues.length; i++) {
  for (let j = 0; j < cardSuits.length; j++) {
    const card = { value: cardValues[i], suit: cardSuits[j] };
    randomDeck.push(card);
  }
}
console.log(randomDeck);
```

This code will create a random deck of 52 cards, with 13 card values (Ace, Two, Three, etc.) and 4 card suits (Hearts, Diamonds, Spades, Clubs). The resulting **randomDeck** array will contain 52 card objects, each with a **value** property and a **suit** property.

When I asked it to shuffle the deck, I expected it to use built-in array functions, but it did not. Instead, it wrote a shuffle function the hard way.

```
// Function to shuffle the deck
function shuffleDeck(deck) {
  // Loop through the deck and swap each card with a randomly chosen card
  for (let i = 0; i < deck.length; i++) {
    const randomIndex = Math.floor(Math.random() * deck.length);
    const temp = deck[i];
    deck[i] = deck[randomIndex];
    deck[randomIndex] = temp;
  }
```

```
  return deck;
}
// Shuffle the deck
const shuffledDeck = shuffleDeck(randomDeck);
console.log(shuffledDeck);
```

Encouraged, I asked it one more time, this time instructing it to use built-in array functions. It gave me basically the same function Copilot wrote.

```
// Shuffle the deck using built-in Javascript array functionality
const shuffledDeck = randomDeck.sort(() => Math.random() - 0.5);
console.log(shuffledDeck);
```

That should do the trick. It's all about asking for exactly what you want.

Deck of uno cards

Does they even know what Uno cards are?

Copilot

```
// Create a random deck of Uno cards
const unoDeck = [];
const colors = ['Red', 'Yellow', 'Green', 'Blue'];
const specialCards = ['Skip', 'Reverse', 'Draw Two', 'Wild', 'Wild Draw Four'];
for (const color of colors) {
 for (const rank of ranks) {
   unoDeck.push({ color, rank });
 }
 for (const specialCard of specialCards) {
   unoDeck.push({ color, specialCard });
 }
}
```

It's clear that it knows something about Uno cards, given the colors and special cards. I was a little annoyed that it didn't create the rank. I presume it used the rank array from the last code block, since I didn't delete any of that code.

I decided to delete the other card code and try again.

```
// Create a random deck of Uno cards
const { uno } = require('@faker-js/faker');
const deck = [];
for (let i = 0; i < 108; i++) {
  deck.push(uno.card());
}
```

Nope, this didn't work at all. Not surprisingly, the `faker` library has no `uno` export. Nothing else I tried got it to work. The first code block was actually better.

ChatGPT

I must admit to being impressed with what ChatGPT gave me. It produced functional, well-documented code, and an explanation of what it generated.

```
Create a random deck of Uno cards
// Create an array of all possible card values
const cardValues = ['0', '1', '2', '3', '4', '5', '6', '7', '8', '9', 'Skip', 'Reverse', 'Draw Two', 'Wild', 'Wild Draw Four'];
// Create an array of all possible card colors
const cardColors = ['Red', 'Yellow', 'Green', 'Blue'];
// Create an empty array to store the random deck of Uno cards
const randomDeck = [];
// Loop through each card value and color, creating a new card object and pushing it to the randomDeck array
for (let i = 0; i < cardValues.length; i++) {
  for (let j = 0; j < cardColors.length; j++) {
    // Skip the 'Wild' and 'Wild Draw Four' card values since they can be any color
    if (cardValues[i] === 'Wild' || cardValues[i] === 'Wild Draw Four') {
      continue;
    }
```

```
  const card = { value: cardValues[i], color: cardColors[j] };
  randomDeck.push(card);
 }
}
// Add the 'Wild' and 'Wild Draw Four' cards to the randomDeck array
for (let i = 0; i < 4; i++) {
 const wildCard = { value: 'Wild', color: 'Any' };
 randomDeck.push(wildCard);
}
for (let i = 0; i < 4; i++) {
 const wildDrawFourCard = { value: 'Wild Draw Four', color: 'Any' };
 randomDeck.push(wildDrawFourCard);
}
console.log(randomDeck);
```

This code creates a random deck of 108 Uno cards, with 15 card values (0, 1, 2, etc.) and 4 card colors (Red, Yellow, Green, Blue) and two special cards 'Wild' and 'Wild Draw Four' card, these cards have any color, then it creates a for loop to add 4 cards of 'Wild' and 'Wild Draw Four' for each color and push it to the randomDeck array, the resulting **randomDeck** array will contain 108 card objects, each with a **value** property and a **color** property.

Grocery shopping list

Copilot

This one also used `faker`, and after a few false starts, it finally gave me this:

```
// Create a random grocery list
const groceryList = [];
for (let i = 0; i < 10; i++) {
 groceryList.push(faker.commerce.productName());
}
```

It was more proof that Copilot is aware of the rest of the code in your project.

Sometimes you need to delete the code it generated before and try again. If you don't like what you get, try rewording the comment slightly.

ChatGPT

ChatGPT took a slightly different approach. It seems to understand whether it should take prior instructions into account. When given this prompt, it did exactly what I thought it would.

Create an array of possible grocery items

```
// Create an array of possible grocery items
const groceryItems = ['Apples', 'Bananas', 'Oranges', 'Lemons', 'Lettuce', 'Carrots', 'Potatoes', 'Onions', 'Tomatoes', 'Garlic', 'Ground Beef', 'Chicken Breasts', 'Eggs', 'Milk', 'Cheese', 'Bread', 'Pasta', 'Rice', 'Beans', 'Cereal', 'Yogurt'];

// Create an empty array to store the random grocery list
const randomList = [];

// Function to generate a random number of items
function randomNumberOfItems() {
  return Math.floor(Math.random() * groceryItems.length);
}

// Loop through the groceryItems array and push a random number of items to the randomList array
for (let i = 0; i < randomNumberOfItems(); i++) {
  randomList.push(groceryItems[Math.floor(Math.random() * groceryItems.length)]);
}

console.log(randomList);
```

This code creates an array of possible grocery items, then creates an empty array to store a random grocery list, it also creates a function **randomNumberOfItems** that uses **Math.random()** to generate a random number of items, this function is then used to create a for loop that will push a random number of items to the randomList array. The resulting **randomList** array will contain a random number of grocery items from the **groceryItems** array.

Stock market symbols

Copilot

Copilot made a valiant attempt on this one, but it wanted to use currency symbols from `faker`, which apparently has no stock ticker symbols.

```
// Create a list of random stock symbols
const symbols = [];
for (let i = 0; i < 100; i++) {
  symbols.push(faker.finance.currencyCode());
}
```

It generated a list of 100 3-letter codes. For the purposes of sample code in a demo UI, I suppose this would do the job.

ChatGPT

What I most appreciate about ChatGPT is that it understands context. It knows what I mean by "Stock Symbols." It gave me a very thorough code block.

```
Create a list of random stock symbols
// Create an array of possible stock symbols
const stockSymbols = ['AAPL', 'GOOGL', 'AMZN', 'FB', 'MSFT', 'BABA', 'TATAMOTORS', 'BA', 'INFY', 'WMT', 'GE', 'CVX', 'PG', 'XOM', 'CMCSA', 'C'];

// Create an empty array to store the random stock symbols
const randomStockSymbols = [];

// Function to generate a random number of stock symbols
function randomNumberOfSymbols() {
  return Math.floor(Math.random() * stockSymbols.length);
}

// Loop through the stockSymbols array and push a random number of symbols to the randomStockSymbols array
for (let i = 0; i < randomNumberOfSymbols(); i++) {
  randomStockSymbols.push(stockSymbols[Math.floor(Math.random() * stockSymbols.length)]);
}
```

```
console.log(randomStockSymbols);
```

Random stock price stream

Can they also provide a random price stream from one of those symbols?

Copilot

```
// Create a list of random stock prices
const prices = [];
for (let i = 0; i < 100; i++) {
  prices.push(faker.finance.amount());
}
console.table(prices);
```

Then I figured I'd ask Copilot to put the two lists together.

```
// Combine the prices and symbols into a list of stocks
const stocks = [];
for (let i = 0; i < 100; i++) {
  stocks.push({
    symbol: symbols[i],
    price: prices[i],
  });
}
console.table(stocks);
```

It isn't horrible, but it would be cool to generate a stream that I could subscribe to.

```
// Generate an observable stream of prices for each stock, changing every 5 seconds
const { interval } = require('rxjs');
const { map, mergeMap } = require('rxjs/operators');
const { from } = require('rxjs');
const { zip } = require('rxjs');
const { take } = require('rxjs/operators');

const stockStream = from(stocks);
const priceStream = interval(5000).pipe(take(10));
const combinedStream = zip(stockStream, priceStream).pipe(
```

```
map(([stock, price]) => {
  stock.price = price;
  return stock;
 }
));
combinedStream.subscribe((stock) => {
 console.log(stock);
});
```

This was cool and mostly correct. I would have preferred that it take its prices from the list it created earlier, but it did most of the heavy lifting for me. When I ran it, it emitted a stock symbol and price every 5 seconds.

ChatGPT

The code I got from ChatGPT was similar to what Copilot gave me, but far more complete. As with past prompts, it insists on giving a complete answer to every question. Here is what it gave me in its entirety.

Generate an observable stream of prices for each stock, changing every 5 seconds

```
const { Observable } = rxjs;
```

// Create an array of possible stock symbols

```
const stockSymbols = ['AAPL', 'GOOGL', 'AMZN', 'FB', 'MSFT', 'BABA', 'TATAMOTORS', 'BA', 'INFY', 'WMT', 'GE', 'CVX', 'PG', 'XOM', 'CMCSA', 'C'];
```

// Create an empty array to store the random stock symbols

```
const randomStockSymbols = [];
```

// Function to generate a random number of stock symbols

```
function randomNumberOfSymbols() {
 return Math.floor(Math.random() * stockSymbols.length);
}
```

// Loop through the stockSymbols array and push a random number of symbols to the randomStockSymbols array

```
for (let i = 0; i < randomNumberOfSymbols(); i++) {
```

```javascript
  randomStockSymbols.push(stockSymbols[Math.floor(Math.random() * stockSymbols.length)]);
}
console.log(randomStockSymbols);
// Create an empty array to store the random stock prices
const randomStockPrices = [];
// Function to generate a random stock price
function randomStockPrice() {
  return (Math.random() * (300 - 50) + 50).toFixed(2);
}
// Loop through the randomStockSymbols array and push a random stock price to the randomStockPrices array
for (let i = 0; i < randomStockSymbols.length; i++) {
  const stock = {
    symbol: randomStockSymbols[i],
    price: randomStockPrice()
  };
  randomStockPrices.push(stock);
}
console.log(randomStockPrices);
// Create an observable stream for each stock symbol
const stockStreams = randomStockSymbols.map(symbol => {
  return Observable.create(observer => {
    setInterval(() => {
      observer.next({
        symbol,
        price: randomStockPrice()
      });
```

```
    }, 5000);
  });
});
// Subscribe to each stock stream and log the updated stock price
stockStreams.forEach(stream => {
  stream.subscribe(stock => {
    console.log(`${stock.symbol}: $${stock.price}`);
  });
});
```

This code generates an observable stream for each stock symbol in the **randomStockSymbols** array, using the **rxjs** library and the **Observable.create()** method. It uses the **setInterval()** function to emit a new stock object containing the symbol and a random price every 5 seconds. Then it subscribes to each stock stream and logs the updated stock price.

It's important to note that for this code to work, you should import **rxjs** library first.

You have to admit that's pretty complete.

Conclusion

Overall, I rate Copilot a 5 or 6 out of 10 on the success scale. It ended up being more of a helper to use the `faker` library than anything. I suppose that even though it didn't do what I expected it to do, it really doesn't matter how the sample data is generated. Copilot uses the tools at its disposal, which is a good thing. I don't think this should count against Copilot, though. It does a great job, considering what it's designed to do.

ChatGPT, on the other hand, scored an 8 or a 9. It will use or not use existing libraries, which makes it more flexible. It also remembers past requests, so you can give it instructions such as, "Do that again, using single quotes instead of double quotes." Or "Rewrite that function using built-in JavaScript array functions." One downside of ChatGPT that I did not show is that every time you ask it to rewrite or refactor an earlier answer, it slowly regenerates the entire block. After five or six of those, the time it takes to generate its answers feels longer and longer.

I did discover later that ChatGPT Plus, the paid subscription version, generates code much faster. I guess that's what you get for $20/month (price as of March 2023).

As we continue to explore the various ways to use these tools, I think you'll agree that each has its strengths, depending on where and how it's used.

AGILE PROJECT MANAGEMENT

Image by 14995841 from Pixabay

I'm going to make an admission here. I am not a fan of project management tasks. I don't like creating stories, grooming stories, doing project estimates, etc. I want to build working code and do it as fast as possible.

However, I do recognize the value of project management tasks. That's where AI comes into play. AI can help make the process a little simpler and more pleasant by automating certain aspects of the project management process. For example, AI-powered tools can assist with story grooming by creating comprehensive user acceptance criteria.

This gets these tasks off my plate as quickly as possible, so that I can get to the more interesting job of delivering software. In this chapter, I'll show you how I use ChatGPT for project planning.

Note, GitHub Copilot is not really suitable for this type of usage, but I'll get back to using it when it's time to write some code.

Project Concept

I started by describing an application to ChatGPT. The application in question is the demo application from many of books and video courses.

> *The application will store and manage the attendance for a single classroom. It will store the names and contact information for the class roster and the students' parents. It will provide a way to add, edit, and remove students, as well as the ability to mark the students absent or present for a given day. The app will run on both desktop web, iOS, and Android. It will also connect to the device's camera to add a photograph of each student.*

I gave that description to ChatGPT and asked it "to write a marketing summary for it." Here is its reply.

> "Attendance Manager" is a multi-platform app that simplifies classroom attendance management. With its easy-to-use interface, you can quickly store and manage the names, contact information, and attendance records of students and their parents. The app features a photo capturing capability, which makes student identification quick and effortless. Whether you are on a desktop computer or a mobile device, Attendance Manager ensures that you have access to your class roster and attendance records anytime, anywhere. Experience the ease and convenience of attendance management with Attendance Manager!

How great is that!? Beginning with a dry application description, I got a decent description suitable for use as a starting point for a market brochure. More importantly for my purposes is that I can then build on that to help with the rest of the project plan.

Epics and User Stories

Next, I asked ChatGPT to use that description to generate my epics and user stories for this admittedly simple application.

> *Given that description, create a few agile epics that will help direct the development of the application. I envision three different visual screens for the application. A home page, a roster page, and a student details page. Add those to the epics and stories.*

Student Information Management:

Epic: Manage Student Information

- As a teacher, I want to be able to add, edit, and remove students and their parents' contact information in the system.
- As a teacher, I want to be able to view a class roster and search for specific students.

Story: Create Student Details Page

- As a teacher, I want to navigate to the student details page from the roster page to add, edit, or remove student information.
- As a teacher, I want to view a student's photo, name, and contact information on the student details page.

Attendance Management:

Epic: Manage Student Attendance

- As a teacher, I want to be able to mark students as absent or present for a given day.
- As a teacher, I want to view the attendance records for a specific date range or for an individual student.

Story: Create Roster Page

- As a teacher, I want to view the class roster and mark students as absent or present on the roster page.
- As a teacher, I want to view the attendance records for each student on the roster page.

Multi-platform Support:

Epic: Ensure Cross-platform Compatibility

- As a teacher, I want to use the application on a desktop computer, iOS device, or Android device.
- As a teacher, I want the application to have a responsive design that adjusts to different screen sizes.

Story: Create Home Page

- As a teacher, I want to view the class roster and navigate to the roster and student details pages from the home page.
- As a teacher, I want the home page to display on all devices with a responsive design.

Photo Capturing:

> **Epic: Associate Photos with Student Profiles**
> - As a teacher, I want to take photos of students using the device's camera and associate the photos with their respective profiles.
> - As a teacher, I want to be able to view the photos of students when I am marking attendance or viewing the class roster.
>
> **Story: Add Photo Capturing Capability**
> - As a teacher, I want to be able to access the device's camera from the student details page to take photos of students.
> - As a teacher, I want to be able to associate a photo with a student's profile on the student details page.

This is more than I would have come up with on my own, and the user stories are easily good enough to get started planning the project. Keep in mind that this took a only a few seconds.

Next, let's see what happened when I asked for some user acceptance criteria for these stories. I won't show them all here, just enough to give you an idea of what it does.

> *Generate some user acceptance criteria for the stories in epic 1 using the "given, when, then" syntax*
>
> **Manage Student Information - Create Student Details Page**
>
> Given that I am a teacher using the application, when I navigate to the student details page from the roster page, then I should see an interface to add, edit, or remove student information.
>
> Acceptance Criteria:
> - The student details page is accessible from the roster page.
> - The interface displays the student's photo.
> - The interface includes fields for the student's name, contact information, and photo.
> - The interface allows the teacher to add a new student, edit existing student information, and remove a student.
> - The changes made in the interface are saved in the system.
>
> **Manage Student Information - View Class Roster**
>
> Given that I am a teacher using the application, when I view the class roster, then I should see a list of all students in the class and their contact information.
>
> Acceptance Criteria:

- The class roster is accessible from the home page.
- The roster displays the student's photo, name, and contact information.
- The roster allows the teacher to search for a specific student.
- The roster is sorted alphabetically by student name.
- Manage Student Information - Search for Specific Students

Given that I am a teacher using the application, when I search for a specific student on the class roster, then I should see the matching students and their contact information.

Acceptance Criteria:

- The teacher can initiate a search on the class roster page.
- The search matches the student name, photo, and contact information with the search query.
- The search results are displayed in a list format.
- The search results are sorted alphabetically by student name.

ChatGPT took care of one of the most tedious tasks in software development, at least from where I'm sitting. Is it perfect? Not at all. There are features and acceptance criteria I never asked for. I didn't say anything about a search feature, but ChatGPT added it to my application. That doesn't mean I have to add it.

There are a couple of ways to look at this. One is that it just suggested a feature I hadn't considered, but maybe should. The other is that I can simply ignore it or ask ChatGPT to regenerate the UAC without the search feature. Either way is a win for me.

It also didn't write each of the acceptance criteria using "Given/when/then," but otherwise I'm happy with what it gave me.

By the way, I did ask it to generate UAC without using the term "user acceptance criteria." It tried to create "user access control" instead, which was a very different result.

Estimations

If there is a task most developers dislike more than generating stories and acceptance criteria, it would have to be estimations. Fortunately, I was able to get ChatGPT to manage that for me as well, at least partially, using T-Shirt sizing.

T-Shirt Sizing

In case you aren't familiar with the concept, T-Shirt sizing is a method of estimation that assigns relative sizes to tasks or features based on their perceived level of difficulty. The sizing is usually done using a set of labels, such as XS (extra small), S (small), M (medium), L (large), XL (extra-large), and so on, to indicate the relative size of each task.

The exact labels and their meanings may vary between organizations, but the goal is to provide a rough, relative estimate that can be used for planning and prioritization purposes. The method is named after the idea of T-shirts being different sizes, with a small T-shirt being easier to handle than a large one.

With that understanding, I asked ChatGPT:

> *Given the relative difficulties of those tasks and their UAC, generate a rough relative estimate for each using T-shirt sizing.*
>
> Manage Student Information - Create Student Details Page
>
> Size: Medium
>
> The task of creating the student details page involves adding and editing student information, which is relatively straightforward but requires a user-friendly interface. The user acceptance criteria (UAC) also include saving changes made in the interface, which requires a functional back-end. Therefore, this task is estimated to be a medium-sized task.
>
> Manage Student Information - View Class Roster
>
> Size: Small
>
> The task of creating the class roster page involves displaying a list of students and their contact information, which is a relatively simple task. The UAC includes sorting the list alphabetically and allowing the teacher to search for specific students, which are additional features that can be added with minimal effort. Therefore, this task is estimated to be a small-sized task.
>
> Manage Student Information - Search for Specific Students
>
> Size: Small
>
> The task of adding a search functionality to the class roster page involves matching student information with the search query and displaying the results. This is a relatively simple task that can be implemented with minimal effort. Therefore, this task is estimated to be a small-sized task.

What impressed me about the response is that it attempted to justify its estimates. With this as a starting point, I would feel a lot more comfortable creating some estimates for management. If nothing else, it gives the team a place to begin a longer discussion.

Fibonacci Estimates

While T-Shirt Sizing is often enough for the development team, management typically wants something a little more concrete. My team uses Fibonacci values.

The idea behind using Fibonacci numbers is that each number represents a rough estimate of the amount of effort required to complete a task or feature, and the gap between each number becomes progressively larger as the estimate becomes larger. This helps to avoid the use of overly precise estimates, which can be difficult to achieve and lead to unachievable expectations.

This method allows for the estimation of tasks with a high degree of uncertainty, where the exact effort required is not known. By using a set of standardized values, teams can make rough estimates that are consistent and easily understood across the organization.

I asked ChatGPT to rewrite its T-Shirt estimates as Fibonacci instead. It generated almost the same text as before, but with different values. I'm showing just those values here.

Manage Student Information - Create Student Details Page

Estimate: 5

Manage Student Information - View Class Roster

Estimate: 3

Manage Student Information - Search for Specific Students

Estimate: 2

Did you spot the difference? Using T-Shirt sizing, the estimates were "medium," "small," and "small." Using Fibonacci values, ChatGPT decided that searching for students was a little simpler than viewing the class roster.

That type of awareness is common for developers, but I didn't expect it from the AI.

Summary

ChatGPT can be used to write concise and clear marketing summaries, create agile epics and user stories, generate user acceptance criteria, and provide rough estimates. It can help streamline the process by providing fast and accurate responses. The use of ChatGPT in in this way can help you achieve greater efficiency and consistency, especially if (like me) you don't particularly care for these tasks.

I've been using this strategy personally and as a result, I'm enjoying the process more than ever before. I find staring at a blank screen to be hard, but I don't mind rephrasing and refining the output ChatGPT gives me for these tasks.

LET'S BUILD AN APP!

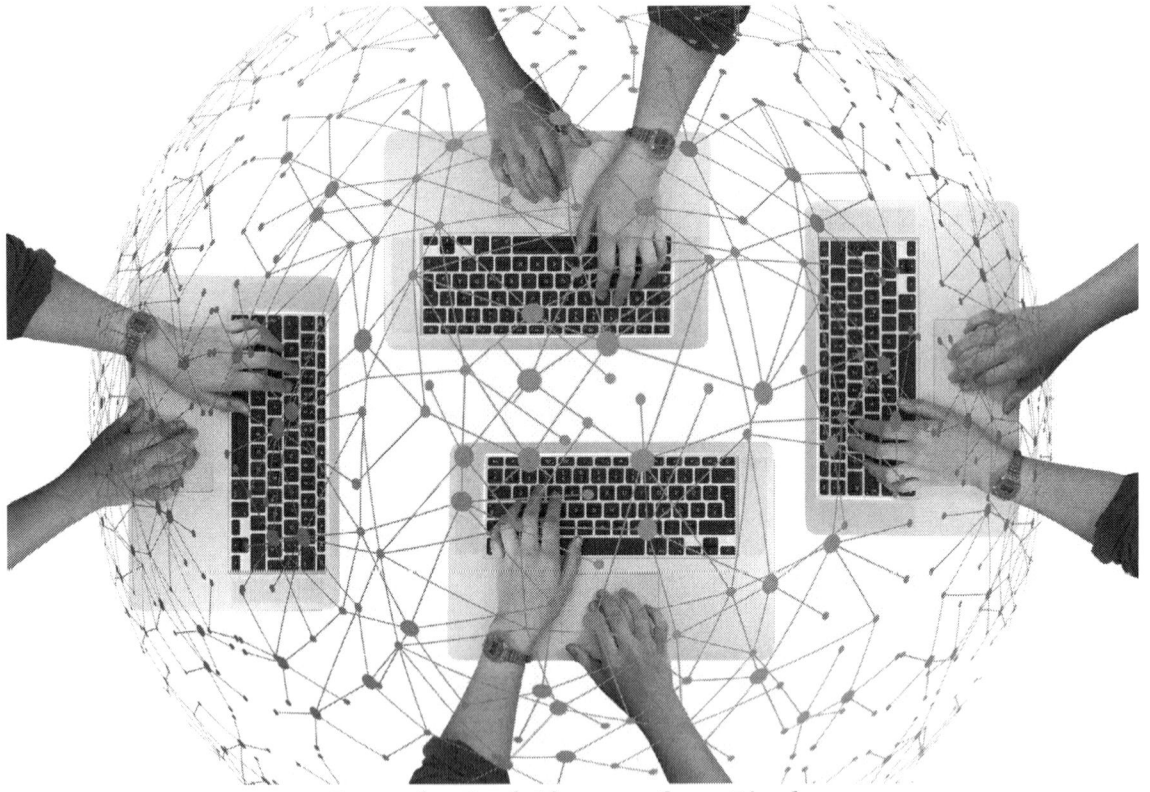

Image by Gerd Altmann from Pixabay

In the previous chapters, I included very verbose output from both Copilot and particularly ChatGPT. I also showed the output from each tool to show how well or poorly it did with the given prompts.

For this chapter, I'm going to use Copilot as my pair programming companion to build a modest application.

My technology stack will be a web application with HTML, Angular, and the Ionic Framework. Those choices are tangential to the point of using AI as my companion. Those are what I use every day, so I will quickly know whether or not the code generated by the AI is accurate.

It won't be a complicated app, just enough to demonstrate how I use the tools.

Hopefully you will follow along. If you do, let me know how it goes.

An Ionic App

Ionic is a popular web framework for building applications of all types, but it has traditionally been used to create hybrid mobile applications. That is, mobile apps written with web technologies.

New Blank Ionic Angular Application

To prepare for this project, I made sure I was on the latest version of Ionic with `npm i -g @ionic/cli`. Then created a brand new, blank Ionic-Angular app with `ionic start`.

Once the project was created, I opened it in VS Code. I then created a blank text file and told VS Code that it's a Shell script file. If you have been reading along, you may suspect what I was about to do.

Add a New Ionic Page

I couldn't remember how to create a new page (well, I could, but I wanted to see whether Copilot also knew). In my new Shell script file, I entered the following comment and waited to see what Copilot would offer me.

```
# Create a new ionic page called Posts
ionic g page Posts
```

That command is one of a few valid ways to create a page, so I ran it in VS Code's built-in terminal. Once created, I opened the app.component.html file, so that I could add a menu to my new page.

Side Menu and Split Pane

Whenever I create a new Ionic app, I start with a blank template, even though I know I'm going to want a side menu and a split-pane layout. I don't start with the side-menu template because it adds a bunch of stuff I have to delete. The drawback is that I truly can never remember everything I need to do to create the split-pane and the side-menu. I was confident that Copilot could handle it, though.

When I opened the HTML file, it looked like this:

```
<ion-app>
  <ion-router-outlet></ion-router-outlet>
</ion-app>
```

Nothing surprising. I removed the `<ion-router-outlet>` line, replacing it with a comment:

```
<!-- Add a side menu and an ion split pane -->
```

Copilot "thought" a moment, almost long enough that I worried that it wasn't working. Then, it gave me three different options. The first option contained two hard-coded pages. The second and third options built a menu from an array of pages on the component. The only difference between the two were some spacing, so I just picked one.

This is what Copilot gave me:

```
<ion-app>
  <!-- Add a side menu and an ion split pane -->
  <ion-split-pane>
    <ion-menu side="start" contentId="main-content">
      <ion-header>
       <ion-toolbar>
        <ion-title>Menu</ion-title>
       </ion-toolbar>
      </ion-header>
      <ion-content>
       <ion-list>
        <ion-menu-toggle auto-hide="false" *ngFor="let p of appPages">
         <ion-item [routerDirection]="'root'" [routerLink]="[p.url]">
          <ion-icon slot="start" [name]="p.icon"></ion-icon>
          <ion-label>
           {{p.title}}
          </ion-label>
         </ion-item>
        </ion-menu-toggle>
       </ion-list>
```

```
    </ion-content>
  </ion-menu>
  <ion-router-outlet id="main-content"></ion-router-outlet>
</ion-app>
```

If you are more astute than I am, you'll notice that the `<ion-split-pane>` tag isn't closed. Copilot waited for me to enter a blank line just before the closing `</ion-app>` tag. Once I did, Copilot finished up for me by adding `</ion-split-pane>`.

My component did not yet have an `appPages` array, so I needed to get Copilot to make one for me. Over in `app.component.ts`, near the top of the class, I entered the word `appPages` as a hint to see what it would do. It gave these lines to me one at a time, meaning I had to accept each suggestion by pressing the `tab` key and continuing by pressing the `return` key.

```
appPages = [
  {
    title: 'Home',
    url: '/home',
    icon: 'home'
  },
```

I did have to cycle through the options when I got to the `url`. It initially suggested `/inbox` for the `url`. `/home` was its second suggestion. You can also see that at this point, it hadn't completed the array. It was waiting for me to give it permission to continue.

I still needed a menu to my new Posts page, so I gave it permission by pressing `return`. It gave me this:

```
  {
    title: 'List',
```

I didn't want that title, but there were no other options. Knowing by now that I can influence Copilot by changing its suggestions and then moving on, I changed the title to `Posts` and moved to the next line. It then added these lines:

```
    url: '/posts',
    icon: 'list'
```

```
},
```

Now I had no more pages, but Copilot would keep adding more if I let it, so I manually closed the array by typing `];` on the next line.

At this point, I hadn't actually checked to see whether any of this code worked but remembered that I had used `npm start` right after opening the project. I switched to my browser where the project was rendered and found this waiting for me:

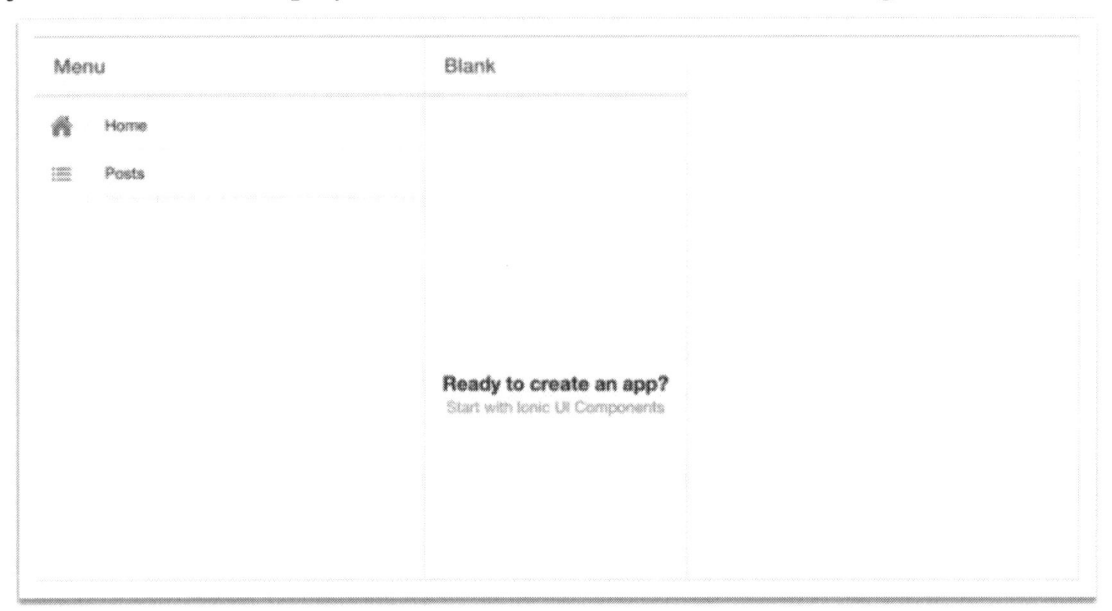

Ionic split-pane app written mostly by GitHub Copilot

Clicking the menus switched to the selected page, so it worked!

Looking at that screenshot, you may see the other oversight that Copilot missed. I admit I missed it at first but want to include it for completeness. The split pane layout isn't working quite right. That home page should take up the full width of the screen.

Looking again at the code, I realized that Copilot did not add the required `contentId` attribute to the `<ion-split-pane>`. Hoping it would offer to do so, I added a blank line before the closing `>` and waited… and waited… nothing.

So, I think I finally stumped Copilot. I manually updated the line to look like this, and then it started working as expected.

```
<ion-split-pane contentId="main-content">
```

Copilot correctly added the `contentId` to the `<ion-menu>`, just not the `<ion-split-pane>`. Weird.

Let's Get Some Data!

If you've been following along in order, you may recall that I had Copilot write me some RxJS with the Angular HttpClient. I will use some of that code here, as it has already been written.

I created a new service with this command:

```
ionic g service ApiService --skip-tests
```

> Yes, I skipped creating tests—I'll deal with Copilot and unit tests later.

I then pasted the following code from the RxJS chapter into the new file.

```typescript
import { Injectable } from '@angular/core';
import { HttpClient } from '@angular/common/http';

// Provide service in root
@Injectable({
  providedIn: 'root'
}) export class ApiService {
  constructor(private http: HttpClient) { }

  // Get all posts from the API
  getAllPosts() {
    return this.http
      .get('https://jsonplaceholder.typicode.com/posts');
  }
}
```

There is more code, but that was enough for my purposes. With this code, I expected I would be able to finish my modest app.

Load Blog Posts from Posts Component

With the service created, it was time to turn my attention to the Posts Component and load those posts into it. I opened `posts.page.ts` and added a hint to the top of the class. Remember, my goal was to write as little code as possible.

```
// Inject ApiService
constructor(private apiService: ApiService) { }
```

Copilot added the constructor, even though I already had one. In this case, it was easy enough to delete the existing one, but what if I already had one with other services in it? I decided to try again with the existing constructor. So, I started with this:

```
// Inject ApiService
constructor(private http: HttpClient) {
}
```

I wanted to give it an existing constructor with parameters in the hopes it wouldn't create a new one. I typed a comma followed by a `[space]` after the `HttpClient`. Copilot added the second parameter correctly, which left me with this:

```
constructor(private http: HttpClient, private apiService: ApiService) { }
```

The service name was correct, but as I have pointed out previously, Copilot won't automatically import the service. Well, it will, but you have to put your cursor on one of the existing imports and then let it figure it out from there, which it will almost always do correctly, except apparently in this case. It wouldn't add it for me, so I just got VS Code to do it instead.

Next, I needed to get those posts. Intellisense is really all that's required in this situation, but again, my goal is to write as close to no code as possible.

```
// Get the posts from the API as an observable.
posts: any;

ngOnInit() {
  this.apiService.getAllPosts().subscribe(data => {
    this.posts = data;
  });
}
```

That is not at all what I wanted, though I can't say it won't work. I deleted that code and tried a different approach. I left the comment but added `posts$ =` and then let

Copilot suggest the rest. This tells Copilot that I want an observable assigned to the variable `posts$`.

```
// Get the posts from the API as an observable.
posts$ =
this.apiService.getAllPosts();
```

That is what I wanted, and all I needed for this file.

Responsive View for Blog Posts

I've always been a big fan of the `<ion-card>`, so I wanted to use a bunch of them to display the blog posts from the above API call. I also want the UI to be responsive, so that was also a requirement.

I switched over to the template file at `posts.page.html` and placed my cursor on the blank line inside the `<ion-content>`.

Given a single HTML comment, this is what I ended up with.

```html
<!-- Create a responsive layout with ion-grid -->
<ion-grid>
 <ion-row>
  <ion-col size="12" size-md="6" size-lg="4" *ngFor="let post of posts">
   <ion-card>
    <ion-card-header>
     <ion-card-title>{{post.title}}</ion-card-title>
    </ion-card-header>
    <ion-card-content>
     <p>{{post.body}}</p>
    </ion-card-content>
   </ion-card>
  </ion-col>
 </ion-row>
</ion-grid>
```

I had no idea it would offer the `<ion-card>`, but as that is what I wanted, I was cool with it. The only thing it got wrong was the `posts` variable, which doesn't exist. I wondered whether it would have been one of the alternative suggestions, so I undid the edit and tried again, planning to cycle through the suggestions. None of its other suggestions fixed that, though, so I tried one other idea.

I changed the comment to reference the actual variable name of `posts$`. Copilot then gave me this. I've found that if you give Copilot enough of a hint, it will get things right.

```html
<!-- Create a responsive layout of posts$ with ion-grid -->
<ion-grid>
 <ion-row>
  <ion-col size="12"
    size-sm="6"
    size-md="4"
    size-lg="3"
   *ngFor="let post of posts$ | async">
   <ion-card>
    <ion-card-header>
     <ion-card-title>{{post.title}}</ion-card-title>
    </ion-card-header>
    <ion-card-content>
     <p>{{post.body}}</p>
    </ion-card-content>
   </ion-card>
  </ion-col>
 </ion-row>
</ion-grid>
```

That's what I wanted! Thinking this might be right, I decided to switch over to the browser to check out my (uh, Copilot's) handiwork.

To my surprise, it compiled but did not run. Did you catch the problem? Maybe if I show you the console error it will become clear.

```
ERROR Error: Uncaught (in promise): NullInjectorError: R3InjectorError(PostsPageModule)[HttpClient -> HttpClient -> HttpClient -> HttpClient]: 
  NullInjectorError: No provider for HttpClient!
```

Oh, right!

I forgot to add the `HttpClientModule` in my app module. Long story short, I could have done it myself, but thought it would better to keep letting Copilot guess what I wanted from my comments. At the top of `app.module.ts`, I added this comment. Copilot added the rest.

```
// Import the HttpClientModule
import { HttpClientModule } from '@angular/common/http';
```

Then in the `imports` array:

```
// Add the HttpClientModule to the imports array
  HttpClientModule,
```

Now it was finally time to review the browser again.

Blog posts app in Ionic Framework written almost entirely by GitHub Copilot

It's even responsive.

Responsive version has only two columns of content and no side menu.

But you may have noticed an oversight. The side menu appropriately disappears on smaller screen widths, but there is no menu button. Did Copilot forget that or did I? Honestly, I'm not sure.

It isn't hard to fix, though, which we'll soon see.

Toolbar Buttons

The last thing I wanted to do was see whether I could get Copilot to make some buttons for me. On the Posts page, the existing header looks like this:

```
<ion-header>
 <ion-toolbar>
  <ion-title>Posts</ion-title>
 </ion-toolbar>
</ion-header>
```

Now, I happen to know where the button goes, but let's assume I do not. What if I were to remove the entire header and see what Copilot would do? I did exactly that, replacing the header with a comment, after which Copilot provided me with the rest.

```
<!-- Header with title and menu button -->
<ion-header>
 <ion-toolbar>
  <ion-buttons slot="start">
   <ion-menu-button></ion-menu-button>
  </ion-buttons>
```

```
    <ion-title>Posts</ion-title>
   </ion-toolbar>
 </ion-header>
```

It did not suggest a Back button, so I added a comment immediately after the menu button.

```
<!-- Back Button -->

    <ion-back-button defaultHref="/home"></ion-back-button>
```

That was the second suggestion. The first one had the back button commented out and no `defaultHref`, which is an attribute that tells Ionic where to navigate if there is nothing "to go back to."

To be consistent, I also needed to do the same thing to the home page. What stood out to me about that, though, is that it this time it remembered the back button and added it automatically.

Copilot tends to recognize patterns in your code and applies those patterns where they make sense.

```
<!-- Header with title and menu button -->
<ion-header>
 <ion-toolbar>
  <ion-buttons slot="start">
   <ion-menu-button></ion-menu-button>
   <!-- Back Button -->
   <ion-back-button defaultHref="/home"></ion-back-button>
  </ion-buttons>
  <ion-title>Posts</ion-title>
 </ion-toolbar>
</ion-header>
```

Not always, though. It did get the page title wrong, so I fixed that manually.

Whether or not the Back button makes sense for the user experience is something we can debate another time.

What about ChatGPT?

Could ChatGPT have done a better job? My initial hesitation about using ChatGPT for this chapter is twofold:

1. There is a lot of back-and-forth when coding. If you're in and out of the editor, back to ChatGPT, etc. It gets tiresome quickly.
2. ChatGPT doesn't know about anything past September 2021. What versions of Angular and Ionic were current then? I decided to ask ChatGPT to find out.

> *What is the newest version of Angular and Ionic Framework you know of?*

As of my knowledge cutoff date of September 2021, the newest versions of Angular and Ionic Framework were:

Angular: The newest version of Angular at that time was version 13, which was released on November 10, 2021.

Ionic Framework: The newest version of Ionic Framework at that time was version 6, which was released on February 11, 2021.

However, please note that software versions are constantly updated and new versions may have been released since my knowledge cutoff date.

Well, I know those versions are current enough that the code it generates should be fine, so I decided to make the most comprehensive prompt I could think of and see what it would give me. Here it is in its entirety.

> *Using Angular and the Ionic Framework, create a complete web application that uses a split-pane layout with a side menu and a default Home page. It should have an Angular service to load blog posts from a remote sample API. Those blog posts should be displayed on a page called Posts. The Posts page should be responsive, displaying the blog post titles and body in an <ion-card>. When working with Observables, prefer the async pipe over subscribing and unsubscribing. Make sure you provide the Ionic CLI commands to create the application and any additional items needed to create the application.*

As an AI language model, I am not able to create full web applications with code. However, I can provide you with a detailed outline of the steps and code snippets needed to complete the requested task.

To create the application using Angular and the Ionic Framework, follow these steps:

1. Install the Ionic CLI by running the following command:

```
npm install -g @ionic/cli
```

2. Create a new Ionic Angular project using the following command:

```
ionic start myapp --type=angular
```

3. Change into the newly created project directory:

```
cd myapp
```

4. Generate a service to load blog posts from a remote sample API by running the following command:

```
ionic generate service services/post
```

5. In the generated post service file (post.service.ts), add the following code to import HttpClient and Observable:

```
import { HttpClient } from '@angular/common/http';

import { Observable } from 'rxjs';
```

6. Add the following code to the post service file to load the blog posts from the remote API:

```
constructor(private http: HttpClient) {}

getPosts(): Observable<any> {

return this.http.get('https://jsonplaceholder.typicode.com/posts');

}
```

7. Generate a new page called Posts by running the following command:

```
ionic generate page pages/posts
```

8. In the generated posts page file (posts.page.ts), add the following code to import the post service and Observable:

```
import { PostService } from '../../services/post/post.service';

import { Observable } from 'rxjs';
```

9. Add the following code to the posts page file to load the blog posts using the post service:

```
posts$: Observable<any>;

constructor(private postService: PostService) {}

ngOnInit() {

 this.posts$ = this.postService.getPosts();

}
```

10. In the posts page template file (posts.page.html), add the following code to display the blog post titles and body in an <ion-card>:

```html
<ion-content>

  <ion-card *ngFor="let post of posts$ | async">

    <ion-card-header>

      {{ post.title }}

    </ion-card-header>

    <ion-card-content>

      {{ post.body }}

    </ion-card-content>

  </ion-card>

</ion-content>
```

11. Modify the app-routing.module.ts file to add routes for the Home and Posts pages:

```typescript
import { NgModule } from '@angular/core';

import { Routes, RouterModule } from '@angular/router';

import { HomePage } from './home/home.page';

import { PostsPage } from './pages/posts/posts.page';

const routes: Routes = [

  {

    path: '',

    component: HomePage

  },

  {
```

```
  path: 'posts',

  component: PostsPage

 }

];

@NgModule({

 imports: [RouterModule.forRoot(routes)],

 exports: [RouterModule]

})

export class AppRoutingModule {}
```

12. Modify the app.component.html file to add a split-pane layout with a side menu and a default Home page:

```
<ion-split-pane>

 <ion-menu>

  <ion-header>

   <ion-toolbar>

    <ion-title>Menu</ion-title>

   </ion-toolbar>

  </ion-header>

  <ion-content>

   <ion-list>

    <ion-item routerLink="/" routerDirection="root">

     Home
```

```
    </ion-item>

    <ion-item routerLink="/posts" routerDirection="root">

      Posts

    </ion-item>

   </ion-list>

  </ion-content>

 </ion-menu>

 <ion-router-outlet></ion-router-outlet>

</ion-split-pane>
```

13. Run the following command to start the application in a local development server:

```
ionic serve
```

This will launch the application in your default web browser.

With these steps, you should have a complete web application using Angular and the Ionic Framework with a split-pane layout and a side menu. The Home page is the default page, and the Posts page displays blog post titles and body in an <ion-card>. The blog posts are loaded from a remote sample API using an Angular service, and the Posts page is responsive using the async pipe.

Please note that the code snippets provided here are just a starting point and may need to be modified or expanded to meet your specific requirements.

I have to say that's a pretty good start. Did you see what it missed, though? I forgot to ask it to give me a menu and back buttons, so it didn't. It also didn't give me a header bar on the Posts page, and it didn't bother to offer any icons for my menu.

Speaking of the side menu, it completely neglected to give me `contentId` values for the `<ion-split-pane>` and the `<ion-menu>`. I didn't bother entering all that into my app but am reasonably certain it won't run as-is.

This is where Copilot really shines. Copilot often needs some coaxing, but it mostly gets the code right. You can easily delete a line or a function, type a new comment, and quickly get the code you need.

With ChatGPT, you can ask it to refine its response, but it will usually generate everything again. Not only that, but I've seen it generate completely different code on subsequent passes, changing more than you ask it to.

I'm not convinced ChatGPT would have saved me much time here. I find that it works better for writing simple functions and algorithms.

It isn't ready for writing complete apps (yet?).

UNIT TESTING

Image by Gerd Altmann from Pixabay

As developers, we know the importance of unit testing in ensuring the quality and reliability of our software. Yet, we also know the struggles that come with creating effective unit tests - the time and effort required, the complexity of the testing process, and the challenge of ensuring comprehensive coverage. Personally, I have often found myself skipping unit tests in the interest of saving time, only to regret it later when bugs and errors inevitably arise.

In this chapter, we will explore how Copilot and ChatGPT can help ease the pain of creating effective unit tests, by generating test cases for a simple Angular service. Through this process, we will see how these tools can help enhance the unit testing process.

The Service

The service itself is simple enough. I wanted to build a means of setting and retrieving two different unique IDs my app can use when making service calls. The first is a "conversation ID" that will be set as an HTTP header for all network calls for a specific user for a given session. It will not change until the application user manually refreshes the screen, closes the browser, or logs out and back in.

The second is a "correlation ID." This will also get sent with each HTTP call, but it changes with every request. I won't show the network calls, just the service to generate the IDs.

The Service API

There are three primary requirements the service implements.

1. It will give me the same conversation ID whenever I ask, unless one does not exist. In that case, it needs to give me a new one and return it.
2. It will give me a fresh correlation ID every time I request one. I should never get the same ID twice.
3. It will provide a way for me to force a fresh conversation ID.

The implementation will use `UUIDs` for both the `conversationId` and the `correlationId`. In case you aren't aware of the term `UUID`, I asked ChatGPT to define it:

> *What is a UUID?*
>
> A UUID, or Universally Unique Identifier, is a type of identifier that is used to uniquely identify information in a distributed system. A UUID is a 128-bit number represented as a sequence of hexadecimal digits, typically displayed in groups separated by hyphens. UUIDs are designed to be unique across both space and time, meaning that they should never collide or be duplicated, even if generated by different systems at different times. UUIDs are commonly used in a variety of contexts, including as keys in databases, as identifiers for files or objects in storage systems, and as session IDs in web applications. The use of UUIDs helps to ensure that there is no ambiguity or conflict when multiple systems need to refer to the same entity, and also helps to provide an additional layer of security by making it more difficult to guess or manipulate identifiers.

In short, `UUIDs` are perfect identifiers to use for my purposes in identifying and correlating HTTP calls across various systems.

The code itself small and straightforward. I will reproduce the entirety of the service here for reference.

```
import { Injectable } from '@angular/core';
import { v4 as uuidv4 } from 'uuid';
@Injectable({
  providedIn: 'root'
```

```
})
export class CorrelationService {
  conversationId: string = '';
  resetConversationId() {
    this.conversationId = uuidv4();
    return this.conversationId;
  }
  getConversationId() {
    return this.conversationId || this.resetConversationId();
  }
  getCorrelationId() {
    return uuidv4();
  }
}
```

There are three functions:

- `resetConversationId`: creates a brand new `UUID` and assigns it to the internal `coversationId` variable and returns that new value.
- `getConversationId`: returns the internal `conversationId` if it has a value, or calls resetConversationID and returns its result.
- `getCorrelationId`: simply returns a new `UUID` every time it's called.

As I said, it is a very simple service.

The Testing Framework

I want to start by reviewing the test code that is automatically generated by the Angular CLI. I do not mean for this to be a comprehensive introduction to testing, but I will explain the basics. It should be enough for you to follow along in your own tests.

By default, when you use the Angular CLI to create a service, it will also create a default test file. In my case, it created this for me.

```
import { TestBed } from '@angular/core/testing';
import { CorrelationService } from './correlation.service';
describe('CorrelationService', () => {
  let service: CorrelationService;
  beforeEach(() => {
    TestBed.configureTestingModule({});
    service = TestBed.inject(CorrelationService);
  });
  it('should be created', () => {
    expect(service).toBeTruthy();
  });
});
```

The first `import` line brings in the Angular testing class called `TestBed`. This class contains most of the basic testing framework.

The second pulls in the service to be tested, also known as the "System Under Test," or SUT. This is assigned to the variable `service`.

describe

```
describe('CorrelationService', () => {
```

With most JavaScript testing frameworks, tests are organized into one or more `describe` functions. These functions encapsulate related tests and isolate the inner tests from other, unrelated tests. They can be nested, as you will see shortly.

The `describe` function is called with two parameters.

1. The test label. In this case, the name of the service to be tested.
2. The function that contains the tests themselves. Here it is an arrow function. It contains a single variable representing the service, but nothing is assigned to it yet.

beforeEach

```
beforeEach(() => {
  TestBed.configureTestingModule({});
  service = TestBed.inject(CorrelationService);
});
```

Directly inside this function is another function call, `beforeEach`, which itself contains another arrow function. This function is called by the testing framework before every unit test is executed.

Inside this function is a call to `TestBed.configureTestingModule({})`, and you can see that it is being passed an empty object as its only argument. This object contains the test module's options. It can accept just about every option a normal Angular module can. Most tests use this to configure Angular's dependency injection system to inject test doubles required by the SUT. My service has no dependencies, so there is nothing to configure.

Other Functions

Not shown are some other functions that can contain setup/tear-down instructions:

- `beforeAll`: called once before any tests inside the `describe` are run. This is typically used to set up the state required by all tests, but which won't change from test to test.

- `afterEach`: called after each unit test function in the `describe`. This is used to tear down or reset the state to undo any side effects that a test might have created.

- `afterAll`: called once after all tests in the `describe` have been run. Again, this is used to reset the global state so that effects from your `describe` function don't bleed into others.

it

```
it('should be created', () => {
  expect(service).toBeTruthy();
});
```

This function defines a single unit test. You can create as many `it` functions as you want inside your `describe`. The generated test comes with a single `it` function. Its signature matches that of `describe`, in that it takes a label and a function defining the test.

When combined with its enclosing describe, the `it` functions should read like this:

[describe Label] [it Label]: Pass/Fail

Thus, when you read the one pre-generated test, it should look like this:

CorrelationService should be created: Pass

Consider this phrasing when you create your own tests.

There is a lot more to Angular testing than this, but I wanted to make sure I explained what you would be seeing before I started.

The Tests

With that explanation out of the way, let's look at the tests GitHub Copilot generated. If you are following along, it should be a simple matter of creating a brand new `describe` for each function to be tested. This isn't strictly necessary. It is perfectly legal to put all your tests inside a single `describe`, but I find that doing this way gives Copilot the context it needs to write the tests properly.

I entered the first line below as a hint, and Copilot generated the tests for me.

```
describe('resetConversationId', () => {
  it('should return conversationId', () => {
    service.resetConversationId();
    expect(service.getConversationId()).toBeTruthy();
  });
```

This test simply checks to see whether calling `getConversationId()` returns a truthy, or non-empty value.

```
  it('should return conversationId if it exists', () => {
    service.resetConversationId();
    const conversationId = service.conversationId;
```

```
    expect(service.getConversationId()).toEqual(conversationId);

  });
```

This test calls `getConversationId()` twice, expecting the two values to be identical. If not, the test will fail.

```
  it('should return conversationId if it exists', () => {

    service.resetConversationId();

    const conversationId = service.conversationId;

    expect(service.getConversationId()).toEqual(conversationId);

  });

});
```

No, that isn't a typo. It generated two identical tests. I don't know why. You'll see that sometimes with Copilot. It can be mildly annoying, but the purpose is so that I can write fewer tests manually. In this case, I'm comfortable with the results.

It generated tests that exercise the function appropriately. One simple refactor I could make would be to move the call to service.resetConversationId() into the beforeEach function, guaranteeing it gets called before each test is executed.

Looking at the tests it gave me, I am not convinced I need separate tests for `resetConversationId`, but it would be easy enough to add them.

Let's look now at the tests for `getCorrelationId`. According to the requirements, it should always return a new one every time it's called. For this one, instead of asking Copilot to complete my describe, I used a comment and let it write everything.

```
// Test getCorrelationId

it('should return correlationId', () => {

  expect(service.getCorrelationId()).toBeTruthy();

});
```

It built a single function for me but didn't go any further. In fact, it isn't a very helpful test, but it does pass. Just like before, all it's doing it is ensuring that the function returns a truthy value.

That isn't nearly complete enough, so I tried again. This time, I gave it two more detailed comments.

```
// Test getCorrelationId returns a different value each time
it('should return correlationId', () => {
  const correlationId = service.getCorrelationId();
  expect(service.getCorrelationId()).not.toEqual(correlationId);
});
```

That's a little better. This test is ensuring that calling `getCorrelationId()` twice returns a different value. What if we call it 100 times?

```
// Test getCorrelationId returns a different value a bunch of times
it('should return correlationId', () => {
  const correlationIds = [];
  for (let i = 0; i < 100; i++) {
    correlationIds.push(service.getCorrelationId());
  }
  expect(correlationIds.length).toEqual(100);
  expect(new Set(correlationIds).size).toEqual(100);
});
```

That's a much better test. This test calls `getCorrelationId()` 100 times and checks to see that all 100 results are unique.

I probably would not have thought of using a JavaScript `set` object to ensure that I never get the same value, but it's a clever and elegant solution. Sets cannot contain duplicates. If the set contains 100 values after 100 iterations, then all the generated values were unique.

It just goes to show that Copilot works best with detailed comments.

ChatGPT

What about ChatGPT? In theory, it should be just as good at writing these tests, so let's see what it gives us.

As we have seen throughout the book, the trick to getting ChatGPT to give you decent code is to provide it with the right prompt. For this prompt, it's best to give it the complete service implementation and ask it to write tests using Jasmine (or Jest if you prefer).

> *Given the following Angular service, write a complete suite of unit tests using Jasmine. <I pasted the entire class code here>*

ChatGPT Responded with a complete test suite, as requested.

```
import { CorrelationService } from './correlation.service';
import { v4 as uuidv4 } from 'uuid';
describe('CorrelationService', () => {
  let service: CorrelationService;
  beforeEach(() => {
    service = new CorrelationService();
  });
  it('should create the service', () => {
    expect(service).toBeTruthy();
  });
  describe('resetConversationId()', () => {
    it('should set conversationId to a UUID', () => {
      service.resetConversationId();
      expect(uuidv4.test(service.conversationId)).toBe(true);
    });
    it('should return the new conversationId', () => {
      const conversationId = service.resetConversationId();
      expect(service.conversationId).toEqual(conversationId);
    });
```

```
  });
  describe('getConversationId()', () => {
    it('should return conversationId if set', () => {
      service.conversationId = 'test-id';
      expect(service.getConversationId()).toEqual('test-id');
    });
    it('should call resetConversationId() and return conversationId if not set', () => {
      spyOn(service, 'resetConversationId').and.returnValue('new-id');
      expect(service.getConversationId()).toEqual('new-id');
      expect(service.resetConversationId).toHaveBeenCalled();
    });
  });
  describe('getCorrelationId()', () => {
    it('should return a UUID', () => {
      const correlationId = service.getCorrelationId();
      expect(uuidv4.test(correlationId)).toBe(true);
    });
    it('should return a different UUID each time', () => {
      const correlationId1 = service.getCorrelationId();
      const correlationId2 = service.getCorrelationId();
      expect(correlationId1).not.toEqual(correlationId2);
    });
  });
});
```

Interestingly, these tests don't even compile. While they look reasonable at first glance, two of the tests assume that the uuidv4 library has a test function.

```
expect(uuidv4.test(service.conversationId)).toBe(true);
```

At least the version I am using, v9, it does not.

I commented out those two tests and the rest of them passed.

What's the takeaway here? Using Copilot may be a little more manual, but you have much finer control over what is being generated. With ChatGPT, you get a flood of code that you either have to proofread carefully or accept at face value.

I don't recommend the latter.

Testing HTTP Calls

Testing a simple service is one thing. It's fairly simple and the pattern is straightforward once you've done it a few times. The real value we get from AI is in writing tests for things that aren't necessarily simple and straightforward, like testing HTTP calls.

This is something I know how to do conceptually but can never get the syntax right the first time. For example, I know I must import and use Angular's `HttpClientTestingModule`. There is a certain order that things have to be called and setup that has to be done. And every time, it's an exercise of trial and error until I get it right.

No longer.

I asked ChatGPT to help me write a test for a fictitious weather service. The service itself that I defined looks like this.

```
export class WeatherService {
  http: HttpClient = inject(HttpClient);
  getWeather(zipcode: string) {
    return this.http.get(`weather.com/api/forecast/${zipcode}`);
  }
}
```

ChatGPT gave me a pretty good test suite for this one.

```
import { TestBed } from '@angular/core/testing';
```

```typescript
import { HttpClientTestingModule, HttpTestingController } from '@angular/common/http/testing';
import { WeatherService } from './weather.service';
describe('WeatherService', () => {
  let service: WeatherService;
  let httpMock: HttpTestingController;
  beforeEach(() => {
    TestBed.configureTestingModule({
      imports: [HttpClientTestingModule],
      providers: [WeatherService]
    });
    service = TestBed.inject(WeatherService);
    httpMock = TestBed.inject(HttpTestingController);
  });
  afterEach(() => {
    httpMock.verify();
  });
  it('should be created', () => {
    expect(service).toBeTruthy();
  });
  it('should return the weather for a given zipcode', () => {
    const mockResponse = {
      temperature: 68,
      description: 'Sunny'
    };
    const zipcode = '90210';
    service.getWeather(zipcode).subscribe(response => {
```

```
    expect(response).toEqual(mockResponse);
  });
  const request = httpMock.expectOne(`weather.com/api/forecast/${zipcode}`);
  expect(request.request.method).toBe('GET');
  request.flush(mockResponse);
  });
});
```

It only handled the "happy path," but it gave me the structure I was looking for. As I implied, testing Angular's `HttpClient` is finicky, and I typically get it wrong the first time.

For some reason, I can never seem to remember to include the verification in `afterEach`, which assures that the service only made the expected HTTP calls, no more or less. Nor do I tend to remember the right order to create the mock's `expectOne` and `flush` functions.

Having ChatGPT build this test suite for me saves a lot of time. Once I have the structure in place, I can fill in the gaps (or get Copilot to do it for me).

This test passed the first time, by the way.

Far From Perfect

It's not all wine and roses, to be sure. We have already seen that ChatGPT doesn't know anything past mid-2021 or so. Copilot is better in this regard, as it is trained on almost all of GitHub, plus it can see your code.

I tried to get each of them to help me write a unit test for an Angular `HttpInterceptor`, to use with the `CorrelationService` from the beginning of the chapter. I use an interceptor to add the `correlationId` and `coversationId` values as HTTP headers on every outgoing HTTP call.

ChatGPT knew about the class based `HttpInterceptor`, but nothing about the new functional `HttpInterceptorFn`, which was just introduced in Angular 15. Predictably, ChatGPT knew nothing about it, insisting that no such thing exists.

Copilot tried but gave me nothing I could use. The results are not even worth reproducing here.

Undoubtedly things will get better. For now, consider this one more piece of evidence that as good as the AI gets, we software developers still need to understand our craft. We can use these tools to help us, but we always need to be aware of their limitations.

OTHER CONSIDERATIONS

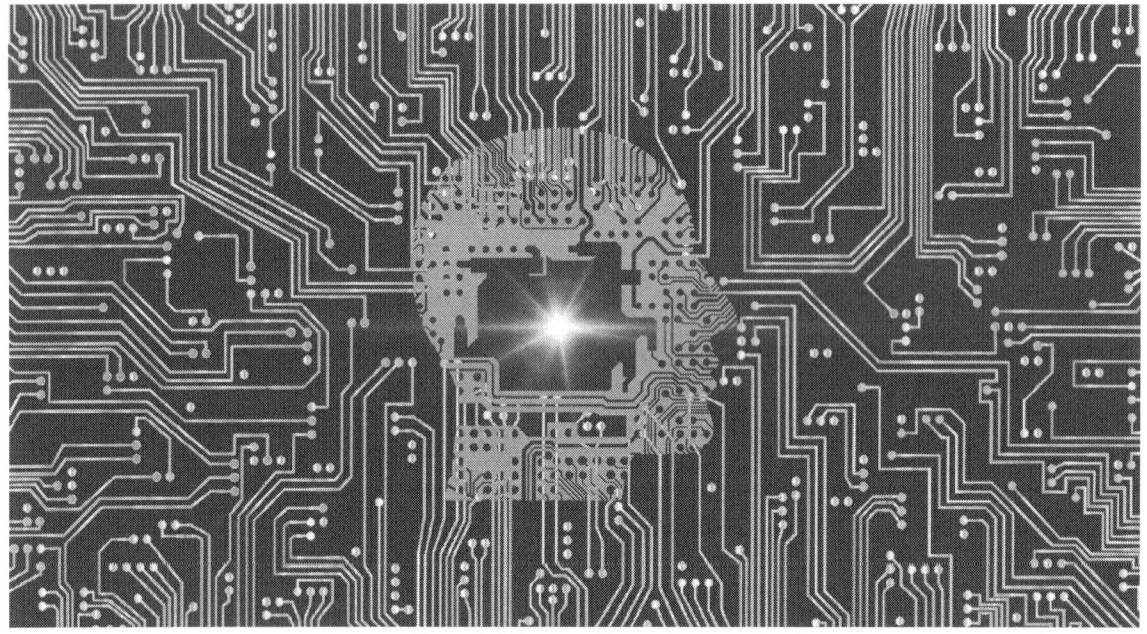

Image by Vicki Hamilton from Pixabay

When writing a book like this, it's hard to know when to stop. I see things on Twitter, people posting about all the cool stuff they're doing with AI. Naturally, I want to try them myself and add them to book. Ultimately, though, such an attitude becomes self-defeating. There are deadlines to meet and other projects the require my attention. I'm sure this isn't the last I'll write about this topic. I already have more ideas going through my head than is probably healthy. I doubt I'll ever get to all of them. However, there are a few interesting uses for AI that don't fit so neatly into any of the prior chapters. I want to take a few moments to touch on them here.

Understanding New Code

Throughout this book, I have been using AI to help with programming tasks. Another possibility is to use it the other way. ChatGPT is especially good at this. Consider the scenario where you have been given some legacy code and you aren't sure what it does (or exactly how). You can paste the code into ChatGPT and ask it for an explanation.

For example, I have some old Ionic/Angular/Firebase code in a project I haven't touched in a while. So, I asked ChatGPT what it does.

```
updateNames() {
 this.db
  .list('/hymns')
  .snapshotChanges()
  .pipe(
   first(),
   switchMap((list) => list)
  )
  .subscribe((hymn) => {
   hymn.payload.child('/arrangements').forEach((arrangement) => {
    const userNameNode = arrangement.child('/user/name');
    const names = userNameNode.val().split(' ');
    const maskedName = `${names[0]} ${names[names.length - 1][0]}.`;
    userNameNode.ref.set(maskedName);
    console.log(maskedName);
   });
   console.log('Done');
  });
}
```

It responded with this explanation:

> This code updates the name property of each user node in the arrangements child nodes of every hymn in the /hymns list of a Firebase Realtime Database.
>
> The code uses the db object (likely an instance of AngularFire2) to access the /hymns list as an

> observable using the list() method. It then calls snapshotChanges() on the observable to get an array of changes in the database, and processes the first change using first().
>
> It then uses switchMap() to flatten the array into an observable of individual changes, which is subscribed to with subscribe().
>
> For each hymn, the code loops through each arrangement node in its arrangements child nodes using the forEach() method.
>
> For each arrangement, the code gets the name property of its user child node, splits the name into an array using the split() method, and creates a masked name consisting of the first name and the first letter of the last name using string interpolation. The masked name is then set as the new value of the name property using the set() method on the userNameNode.ref object.
>
> Finally, the code logs the masked name to the console and repeats the process for each hymn. Once all the hymns have been processed, the code logs 'Done' to the console.

Notice how it correctly inferred the use of both Firebase (AngularFire2) and RxJS.

I then asked ChatGPT about the significance of masking the name. Its response was spot on perfect.

> *What do you believe the significance of the masked name might be?*
>
> The significance of the masked name is likely to protect the privacy of the user's full name.
>
> By masking the name, the code only reveals the first name and the first letter of the last name, which can be useful for anonymizing user data or protecting the user's identity. This can be particularly important if the application is dealing with sensitive information or if the user's full name is not necessary for the functioning of the application.
>
> Using a masked name also helps to maintain consistency in the display of user data. For example, if the application displays a list of users or user-generated content, masking the name can make the display more uniform and visually appealing.
>
> Overall, the use of a masked name is a common technique for protecting user privacy and ensuring a consistent display of user data.

This was a straightforward, almost trivial example. I chose it because it was easy to follow. That said, this technique is particularly useful if you are trying to determine not only what unfamiliar code does, but also why.

Generating Code from Data

Another cool use I have found for ChatGPT is that you can paste some data you get from a web service (or similar) response and ask the AI to convert it into a different data format, or even code that will represent that data's shape.

For example, let's say you have some sample data that looks like this:

```
{
  "contacts": [
    {
      "id": "1",
      "firstName": "John",
      "lastName": "Doe",
      "email": "johndoe@gmail.com",
      "address": {
        "street": "123 Main St.",
        "city": "Anytown",
        "state": "CA",
        "zip": "12345"
      },
      "phones": [
        {
          "type": "home",
          "number": "555-555-5555"
        },
        {
          "type": "work",
          "number": "555-555-5556"
        },
        {
          "type": "mobile",
```

```
      "number": "555-555-5557"
    }
  ]
 }
]
}
```

You can ask ChatGPT to provide you with an interface or a class in the language of your choice. Here is the TypeScript interface it provided:

```
interface Contact {
  id: string;
  firstName: string;
  lastName: string;
  email: string;
  address: Address;
  phones: Phone[];
}
interface Address {
  street: string;
  city: string;
  state: string;
  zip: string;
}
interface Phone {
  type: string;
  number: string;
}
```

I've been favoring JavaScript and TypeScript throughout the book, but just to show that it can and will do more, I asked it to generate a Python object from that data. It gave me this:

```python
class Contact:
    def __init__(self, id, first_name, last_name, email, address, phones):
        self.id = id
        self.first_name = first_name
        self.last_name = last_name
        self.email = email
        self.address = address
        self.phones = phones

class Address:
    def __init__(self, street, city, state, zip_code):
        self.street = street
        self.city = city
        self.state = state
        self.zip_code = zip_code

class Phone:
    def __init__(self, type, number):
        self.type = type
        self.number = number
```

To be honest, I don't know Python, so I can only guess as to its accuracy, but it looks convincing.

Programming Language Translation

Another area where ChatGPT excels is translating code from one language to another. Let's say I am trying to reuse some code from an Angular Service in a React application I'm building. I want to translate the code from a TypeScript class to pure JavaScript.

It's a modest class but will serve as a fine example. Asking ChatGPT to translate it into functional JavaScript yields the following code.

We won't dive into the `MersenneTwister`, other than mention that it's an algorithm for generating random numbers. That's a topic for another day.

```
Given the following TypeScript class, provide me functional JavaScript I can use in its place.
export class ShuffleService {
  random: MersenneTwister = new MersenneTwister();
  seed(slug = 'xyz'): void {
    const hash = this.hashCode(slug);
    this.random.seed = hash;
  }
  hashCode(str: string): number {
    return Array.from(str)
      // eslint-disable-next-line no-bitwise
      .reduce((s, c) => Math.imul(31, s) + c.charCodeAt(0) | 0, 0);
  }
  shuffle(array): any[] {
    return this.random.shuffle(array);
  }
}
```

This is what it came up with.

```
function ShuffleService() {
  const random = new MersenneTwister();
  function seed(slug = 'xyz') {
    const hash = hashCode(slug);
    random.seed = hash;
```

```
}
function hashCode(str) {
 return Array.from(str)
   .reduce((s, c) => Math.imul(31, s) + c.charCodeAt(0) | 0, 0);
}
function shuffle(array) {
 return random.shuffle(array);
}
return {
 seed,
 shuffle,
};
}
```

Framework Translation

It can also help rewrite code from one framework into another. Continuing the example from above, I have a small Ionic-Angular component that I want to reuse in my Ionic-React application. I can simply copy and paste that code and have the new framework code given to me.

Original Ionic-Angular Component

```
<ion-card>
 <ion-card-content>
  <div class="symbols symbols-{{card?.length}}">
   <div class="symbol-wrapper"
    *ngFor="let cardSymbol of card">
    <div class="symbol"
     appRandomRotation>
```

```
    <div appThrottledClick
      [class]="cardSymbol"
      (throttledClick)="onSymbolClick(cardSymbol)"
      [throttleTime]="2000">
      {{cardSymbol}}</div>
    </div>
   </div>
  </div>
 </ion-card-content>
</ion-card>
```

Ionic-React Component from ChatGPT

```
import { IonCard, IonCardContent } from '@ionic/react';
import RandomRotation from './RandomRotation';
import ThrottledClick from './ThrottledClick';
function CardComponent({ card, onSymbolClick }) {
 return (
  <IonCard>
   <IonCardContent>
    <div className={`symbols symbols-${card?.length}`}>
     {card.map((cardSymbol, index) => (
      <div key={index} className="symbol-wrapper">
       <div className="symbol" ref={RandomRotation}>
        <ThrottledClick throttleTime={2000} onClick={() => onSymbolClick(cardSymbol)}>
         <div className={cardSymbol}>{cardSymbol}</div>
        </ThrottledClick>
       </div>
```

```
      </div>
    ))}
   </div>
  </IonCardContent>
 </IonCard>
 );
}

export default CardComponent;
```

> In the above code, we are importing IonCard and IonCardContent components from @ionic/react and using them as the outermost components. The map function is used to iterate over the card array and render the individual symbols. Instead of *ngFor, we are using the map function in JSX to loop over the card array.
>
> For the RandomRotation directive, we need to create a custom React component and attach it as a ref to the symbol element. Similarly, for the ThrottledClick directive, we are creating a custom React component and passing the throttleTime prop and onClick handler as props to it.
>
> Finally, we export the CardComponent component as the default export.

Notice that it recognized the need to extract the Angular directives and let me know that they would need to be created separately. It didn't do that automatically, simply because I didn't provide it with the directives' code.

Angular Material Component from GhatGPT

Or maybe I don't want to use Ionic at all but want to stick with Angular and use the Angular Material components instead.

```
<mat-card>
 <mat-card-content>
  <div [ngClass]="'symbols symbols-' + (card?.length || 0)">
   <div class="symbol-wrapper" *ngFor="let cardSymbol of card">
    <div class="symbol" appRandomRotation>
     <button mat-button appThrottledClick
      [ngClass]="cardSymbol"
```

```
    [throttleTime]="2000"

    (throttledClick)="onSymbolClick(cardSymbol)">

    {{cardSymbol}}

   </button>

  </div>

 </div>

 </div>

 </mat-card-content>

</mat-card>
```

ChatGPT correctly recognized that I can continue to use my Angular directives as-is.

I hope you see how powerful it is to be able to experiment (and even learn) multiple frameworks this way.

Release Notes

ChatGPT can help you generate your software release notes. This one is relatively new for me, and it took me a while to figure out what works best. I tried to start with actual diffs, but ChatGPT doesn't like long passages of text. Instead, I decided to use git commit messages. Here is a sample from an actual project of mine:

```
Add photo (#23)
  * Added capacitor and capacitor storage
  * Converted student service to promises?
  * Fixed DeleteStudent, but not perfectly
  * Removed RxJS from storage service
  * Student CRUD working
  * Added some more functionality
  * Refactored some of the storage code
  * Added New Student functionality
  * Added camera feature
```

> * Standardize state management within the student service (#22)
> * refactor: add explicit modifiers to service signatures
> * refactor: simplify syntax in student service
> * fix: initialize service with stored data
> * refactor: move state changes into student service
> * refactor: use routerLinkActive to determine link state
> * chore: format all files with prettier
> * chore: prefer single quote for strings
> * Added camera feature
> * Made some minor tweeks for the workshop
> * Minor tweaks for conference

I asked ChatGPT to group and prioritize this list into release notes.

> *Given the following string of commit messages for a pull request, generate some release notes, grouped by common themes and sorted by perceived importance. <I pasted the messages here>*
>
> Release Notes
>
> Features
>
> - Added camera feature (#23)
> - Added New Student functionality
> - Added capacitor and capacitor storage
> - Added some more functionality
>
> Fixes
>
> - Fixed DeleteStudent, but not perfectly
> - Removed RxJS from storage service
>
> Improvements
>
> - Standardized state management within the student service (#22)
> - Refactored some of the storage code
> - Refactored the student service to use promises
> - Refactored the student service to simplify syntax
> - Refactored the student service to add explicit modifiers to service signatures
> - Refactored the student service to move state changes into student service
> - Refactored the code to use routerLinkActive to determine link state

- Initialized service with stored data

Miscellaneous

- Made some minor tweaks for the workshop
- Made some minor tweaks for conference
- Formatted all files with prettier
- Preferred single quote for strings

Note: The commit message "Added camera feature" appears twice in the original list, and so it is included only once in these release notes.

It's not perfect, but it provides a great starting point.

Generating Function Documentation

I found a VS Code extension called "Mintlify Doc Writer" that uses AI to generate function-level documentation. It understands multiple languages, including Python, JavaScript, TypeScript, C++, PHP, Java, C#, Ruby, and more.

Once installed, you use it by highlighting function or code block and pressing `Ctrl + .` (period) or `Cmd + .` (period) on the Mac. It will create a comment block above your code appropriate for the language you're using. Here is a sample function from one of my projects and the JSDoc comment it created.

I highlighted the entire function in the editor and pressed `Cmd + .` and watched it work its magic.

```
/**
 * It takes a number of cards and a slug, and returns a deck
 * @param {number} numberOfCards - number - the number of cards in the deck
 * @param [slug] - a string that will be used to seed the random number generator. This is useful if
 * you want to generate the same deck twice.
 * @returns A deck of cards
 */
buildDeck(numberOfCards: number, slug = ''): Deck {
  this.shuffleService.seed(slug);
  this.shuffledSymbols = this.shuffleService.shuffle(SYMBOLS);
  const rawCards = this.dobbleService.dobble(numberOfCards);
```

```
const deck = rawCards.map(card =>
  this.buildCard(card));
return this.shuffleService.shuffle(deck);
}
```

It does a passable job at understanding the meaning of your code and giving you a basic comment. What I find truly useful is combining Mintlify with Copilot to help flesh out your docs even more.

I started with the docs above and pressed Enter to prompt Copilot to flesh them out. Here is the result of the JSDoc comment.

```
/**
 * It takes a number of cards and a slug, and returns a deck of cards
 * The slug is used to seed the random number generator, so that the same deck is generated every time.
 * If no slug is provided, the deck will be generated randomly.
 * @example
 * const deck = deckService.buildDeck(5, 'my-slug');
 * // deck will always be the same
 * @example
 * const deck = deckService.buildDeck(5);
 * // deck will be different every time
 *
 * @param {number} numberOfCards - number - the number of cards you want to generate
 * @param [slug] - a string that will be used to seed the random number generator.
 * @returns A deck of cards
 */
```

It wanted to go further, but I stopped it there, thinking it was detailed enough.

You can find the extension in the VS Code marketplace at https://marketplace.visualstudio.com/items?itemName=mintlify.document

Codeium

About the time I was half finished with the Copilot portions of the book, I got an invitation to try out a new tool like Copilot. It's called Codeium. Like Copilot, it integrates into multiple IDEs, many more than Copilot currently does. The big hook is that it's free for individual users, and they claim it always will be. You can find it at https://codeium.com.

Codeium believes that AI can accelerate all the different "modes" of software development, but rather than having developers install multiple products for each mode, they are building a single product that seamlessly transitions between them. Their latest announcement is natural language-based repo-wide code search, which complements their autocomplete capabilities.

I am not sure why or how they decided to give it away, but it seems like a solid tool that is worth investigating. I look forward to trying it.

THE FUTURE OF SOFTWARE DEVELOPMENT

Image by NoName_13 from Pixabay

Is this the end of software development? Is it time to panic? Should we all pack up our laptops and learn a trade? I don't think so, no. Things will certainly change, but in my experience, these types of changes are usually positive things overall.

AI tools and technologies are having a significant impact on the field of software development. However, I don't believe that they will completely replace software developers in the near future.

As we have seen throughout this book, AI can certainly automate some aspects of software development, such as code generation, testing, and debugging. AI can also assist in the design process, as you saw earlier in the chapter on project management.

Eventually, I believe these tools will be able to help developers analyze code, predict bugs, and provide recommendations for improvements.

Software development is a complex and creative process that involves much more than just writing code. It requires domain knowledge, problem-solving skills, and an understanding of the users' needs. It's not just writing code, but also testing, deployment, maintenance, and updates. AI can certainly help with some of these aspects, but it cannot replace human intelligence and creativity.

In fact, as AI becomes more prevalent in software development, it is likely to create new opportunities and areas for growth. Developers will need to learn how to work with AI tools, understand their limitations, and use them effectively to enhance their own skills and productivity.

While AI will undoubtedly play a significant role in the future of software development, it is unlikely to completely replace the need for human developers. Rather, AI will complement and augment their skills, leading to more efficient and effective software development.

Should You Be Worried?

Should junior developers and people just starting out worry that an AI will take their jobs? Again, I believe the answer is no.

If you are a new, junior level developer or someone who is just starting out in software development, you should not be overly concerned about AI taking your job.

Think of AI like power tools for software development. Just as power tools are designed to make a carpenter's job easier and more efficient, AI tools are designed to make a developer's job easier and more efficient. Power tools allow carpenters to work more quickly, accurately, and safely, and AI tools provide developers with similar benefits.

However, just as power tools don't replace the need for skilled carpenters, AI tools do not replace the need for skilled developers. Both carpenters and developers need to have a deep understanding of their craft, including the underlying principles, best practices, and techniques. They also need to have problem-solving skills and creativity to find new and innovative solutions to the challenges they encounter.

Furthermore, just as power tools require maintenance and upkeep to function properly, AI tools require ongoing development and improvement to stay relevant and effective. Developers need to stay up to date with the latest advancements in AI technology, learn how to use these tools effectively, and adapt their skills as needed.

With the right training, attitude, and mindset, you can build a rewarding and fulfilling career for yourself in software development.

I think we'll look back on this time as one of exciting growth and opportunity. Eventually we'll wonder how we ever got along without these tools.

Amazon Review

If you enjoyed this book, I'd appreciate you leaving me a positive review on Amazon, which you can do here: https://www.amazon.com/review/create-review?asin=B0BSNZFCRM

Updates and Questions

And remember, if you have questions or just want to be updated about this and future books, feel free to sign up at the link above, or send an email to michael@walkingriver.com.

I'm also very active on Twitter, where you can find me posting as @WalkingRiver.

And now, I urge you to go forth and create cool things.

Acknowledgements

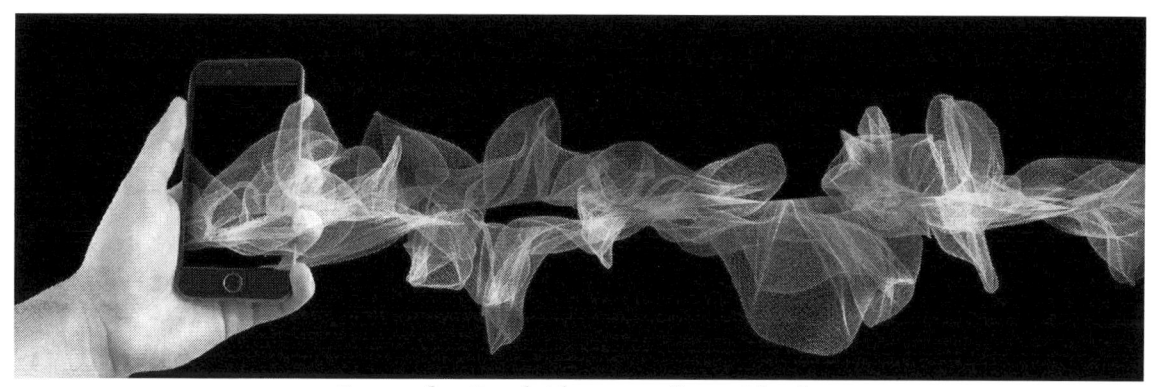

Image by Gerd Altmann from Pixabay

Despite having my name on the cover, this book was a collaborative effort. I am grateful to everyone who contributed their time and sometimes their money to make this book a reality.

Inner Circle

Greg Marine is one of my earliest and most loyal supporters. He is always willing to share a well-considered opinion. He edited and co-authored my book *Don't Say That at Work* and has been with me every step of the way with this book. I couldn't have done it without him. Follow Greg on Twitter at @ByGregMarine and receive a daily dose of optimistic wisdom.

Patrons, Founders, and Ambassadors

The people below pledged more than their time. They pledged their hard-earned cash and I thank for them their faith and support.

Ron Jennings	Mark Goho

Printed in Great Britain
by Amazon